Grief and Loss

**Recent Titles in
Q&A Health Guides**

GRIEF AND LOSS

Your Questions Answered

Louis Kuykendall Jr.

Q&A Health Guides

An Imprint of ABC-CLIO, LLC
Santa Barbara, California • Denver, Colorado

Library of Congress Cataloging-in-Publication Data

Names: Kuykendall, Louis Jr., author.
Title: Grief and loss : your questions answered / Louis Kuykendall Jr.
Description: Santa Barbara : Greenwood, an imprint of ABC-CLIO, LLC, [2020] |
    Series: Q&A health guides | Includes bibliographical references and index.
Identifiers: LCCN 2020007636 (print) | LCCN 2020007637 (ebook) | ISBN
    9781440868009 (print) | ISBN 9781440868016 (ebook)
Subjects: LCSH: Grief. | Loss (Psychology) | Grief in children. |
    Bereavement—Psychological aspects.
Classification: LCC BF575.G7 K88 2020 (print) | LCC BF575.G7 (ebook) |
    DDC 155.9/37—dc23
LC record available at https://lccn.loc.gov/2020007636
LC ebook record available at https://lccn.loc.gov/2020007637

ISBN: 978-1-4408-6800-9 (print)
       978-1-4408-6801-6 (ebook)

24 23 22 21 20   1 2 3 4 5

This book is also available as an eBook.

Greenwood
An Imprint of ABC-CLIO, LLC

ABC-CLIO, LLC
147 Castilian Drive
Santa Barbara, California 93117
www.abc-clio.com

This book is printed on acid-free paper ∞

Manufactured in the United States of America

Contents

Series Foreword

All of us have questions about our health. Is this normal? Should I be doing something differently? Whom should I talk to about my concerns? And our modern world is full of answers. Thanks to the Internet, there's a wealth of information at our fingertips, from forums where people can share their personal experiences to Wikipedia articles to the full text of medical studies. But finding the right information can be an intimidating and difficult task—some sources are written at too high a level, others have been oversimplified, while still others are heavily biased or simply inaccurate.

Q&A Health Guides address the needs of readers who want accurate, concise answers to their health questions, authored by reputable and objective experts, and written in clear and easy-to-understand language.

This series focuses on the topics that matter most to young adult readers, including various aspects of physical and emotional well-being as well as other components of a healthy lifestyle. These guides will also serve as a valuable tool for parents, school counselors, and others who may need to answer teens' health questions.

All books in the series follow the same format to make finding information quick and easy. Each volume begins with an essay on health literacy and why it is so important when it comes to gathering and evaluating health information. Next, the top five myths and misconceptions that surround the topic are dispelled. The heart of each guide is a collection of questions and answers, organized thematically. A selection of five case studies provides real-world examples to illuminate key concepts. Rounding out each volume are a directory of resources, glossary, and index.

It is our hope that the books in this series will not only provide valuable information but will also help guide readers toward a lifetime of healthy decision making.

Acknowledgments

The people I've known who were dying or that dealt with death and loss are numerous. These privileged relationships offered a wide range of perspectives on how to cope with grief and loss and valuable insight regarding how to assist those who are bereaved. One of the memorable connections was with Paul, a young man who was in college when diagnosed with an aggressive brain cancer. Though his illness challenged Paul in every way, he always conveyed an inner courage, wisdom, and faith that belied his years. Paul taught me much about life, death and grief in a relatively short time—treasured lessons I will never forget. I am thankful to him and others who have been patient teachers.

I'm also thankful for seminary professors, colleagues, friends, bereavement experts, authors, researchers, and others who have been willing to share their wisdom and experience about grief and loss. The books read, articles perused, presentations heard and conversations enjoyed have been a tremendous help for this project. Thanks as well to the leaders and members at Zwingli United Church of Christ for their patience, understanding, and much needed support while I was writing.

I am also grateful to my editor, Maxine Taylor, for giving me the opportunity to write and discover more about this topic, and for her patience, insightful suggestions, and skill at what she does. A debt of gratitude to ABC-CLIO and the production team for publishing this book and the health series of which it is a part.

I am especially thankful to my family. My father Louis Sr., mother Elaine, and stepsons Matt, Mark, and Al have given me encouragement, much-needed breaks, and laughter. My daughters Eva and Emily have been incredibly supportive as well. In addition, their life experience and perspective helped shape a few of the entries and some of the wisdom shared is their own. Sally, my wife, has been my inspiration for writing. Her constant reassurance, experience as an author, and inestimable patience and care were, and are, extraordinary gifts.

Truly, no journey should be taken alone.

Introduction

This is a book about hope. Though grief and loss are painful to experience and challenging to talk about, dealing with bereavement is important for everyone, especially teenagers and young adults. Death is often something we fear. Broken relationships can cause deep sorrow. None of us wants to experience pain. However, when tragedies and distressing events occur in our lives, there is much to learn about life and ourselves when we deal with the pain of loss and the emotions that arise when we grieve. Coping with grief and anguish in healthy ways is critical to accepting and adapting to losses and the changes loss brings. Facing grief with courage and support allows for healing and hope to emerge.

This book is written primarily to answer questions about grief and loss, but also to offer suggestions and encouragement for coping, healing, and hope. It's also written because grieving teenagers and young adults have unique needs and ways of handling life's difficulties. The book and its content arise from personal experiences of loss and grief, conversations with those who were dying, meetings with families who suffered loss, as well as the extraordinary wisdom of many bereavement experts, authors, and colleagues. The young people I've known who were dying, or who had to deal with the death of a loved one or friend, have been inspiring teachers. I'm still learning.

Dealing with grief and loss is not a journey to be taken alone. It is important to find people—friends, family, others—and resources that can offer support. Simply finding answers to common questions is a start. However, it's important to know that research and exploration around bereavement is ongoing and changing. Though humans have experienced grief and loss for millennia, there are new things to learn about how people experience bereavement. So, this book expresses just a small fraction of the knowledge and wisdom about bereavement at this point in time, and from a particular perspective. It is impossible to offer in these pages the full breadth of experience, information, and understanding available regarding grief and the many ways teenagers and young adults encounter significant loss. The answers provided are not as in-depth as they could be, but hopefully offer a depth of understanding that will connect the reader to helpful material and insight. There are resources at the end of the book that are valuable for gaining greater perspective and knowledge. Hopefully, the information provided in this work will be a help on the journey, a starting point for greater exploration.

It is inevitable that young people, children, and adults will suffer loss at some point in their lives. How one handles and copes with the loss will be a life-changing experience. With the help of resources like this one, fellow travelers on the journey, the assistance of bereavement professionals, and support from loved ones, friends, and strangers alike, the encounter with grief and loss can lead to healing and hope, a greater appreciation for life, and wisdom needed for the journey ahead.

When this book was in production for publication, the COVID-19 pandemic was quickly reaching startling numbers of cases and deaths. As a result, Question 41, "How is the experience of grief and loss different in a time of a global pandemic, such as the 2019–2020 COVID-19 crisis?" was added before the final version was completed.

Guide to Health Literacy

On her 13th birthday, Samantha was diagnosed with type 2 diabetes. She consulted her mom and her aunt, both of whom also have type 2 diabetes, and decided to go with their strategy of managing diabetes by taking insulin. As a result of participating in an after-school program at her middle school that focused on health literacy, she learned that she can help manage the level of glucose in her bloodstream by counting her carbohydrate intake, following a diabetic diet, and exercising regularly. But, what exactly should she do? How does she keep track of her carbohydrate intake? What is a diabetic diet? How long should she exercise and what type of exercise should she do? Samantha is a visual learner, so she turned to her favorite source of media, YouTube, to answer these questions. She found videos from individuals around the world sharing their experiences and tips, doctors (or at least people who have "Dr." in their YouTube channel names), government agencies such as the National Institutes of Health, and even video clips from cat lovers who have cats with diabetes. With guidance from the librarian and the health and science teachers at her school, she assessed the credibility of the information in these videos and even compared their suggestions to some of the print resources that she was able to find at her school library. Now, she knows exactly how to count her carbohydrate level, how to prepare and follow a diabetic diet, and how much (and what) exercise is needed daily. She intends to share her findings with her mom and her aunt, and now she wants to create a chart that summarizes what she has learned that she can share with her doctor.

Samantha's experience is not unique. She represents a shift in our society; an individual no longer views himself or herself as a passive recipient of medical care but as an active mediator of his or her own health. However, in this era when any individual can post his or her opinions and experiences with a particular health condition online with just a few clicks or publish a memoir, it is vital that people know how to assess the credibility of health information. Gone are the days when "publishing" health information required intense vetting. The health information landscape is highly saturated, and people have innumerable sources where they can find information about practically any health topic. The sources (whether print, online, or a person) that an individual consults for health information are crucial because the accuracy and trustworthiness of the information can potentially affect his or her overall health. The ability to find, select, assess, and use health information constitutes a type of literacy—health literacy—that everyone must possess.

THE DEFINITION AND PHASES OF HEALTH LITERACY

One of the most popular definitions for health literacy comes from Ratzan and Parker (2000), who describe health literacy as "the degree to which individuals have the capacity to obtain, process, and understand basic health information and services needed to make appropriate health decisions." Recent research has extrapolated health literacy into health literacy bits, further shedding light on the multiple phases and literacy practices that are embedded within the multifaceted concept of health literacy. Although this research has focused primarily on online health information seeking, these health literacy bits are needed to successfully navigate both print and online sources. There are six phases of health information seeking: (1) Information Need Identification and Question Formulation, (2) Information Search, (3) Information Comprehension, (4) Information Assessment, (5) Information Management, and (6) Information Use.

The first phase is the *information need identification and question formulation phase*. In this phase, one needs to be able to develop and refine a range of questions to frame one's search and understand relevant health terms. In the second phase, *information search*, one has to possess appropriate searching skills, such as using proper keywords and correct spelling in search terms, especially when using search engines and databases. It is also crucial to understand how search engines work (i.e., how search results are derived, what the order of the search results means, how to use the snippets that are provided in the search results list to select websites, and how to determine which listings are ads on a search engine results page). One also has to limit reliance on surface characteristics, such as the design of a website or a book (a website or book that appears to have a lot of information or looks aesthetically pleasant does not necessarily mean it has good information) and language used (a website or book that utilizes jargon, the keywords that one used to conduct the search, or the word "information" does not necessarily indicate it will have good information). The next phase is *information comprehension*, whereby one needs to have the ability to read, comprehend, and recall the information (including textual, numerical, and visual content) one has located from the books and/or online resources.

To assess the credibility of health information (*information assessment* phase), one needs to be able to evaluate information for accuracy, evaluate how current the information is (e.g., when a website was last updated or when a book was published), and evaluate the creators of the source—for example, examine site sponsors or type of sites (e.g., .com, .gov, .edu, or .org) or the author of a book (practicing doctor, a celebrity doctor, a patient of a specific disease, etc.) to determine the believability of the person/ organization providing the information. Such credibility perceptions tend to become generalized, so they must be frequently reexamined (e.g., the belief that a specific news agency always has credible health information needs continuous vetting). One also needs to evaluate the credibility of the medium (e.g., television, Internet, radio, social media, and book) and evaluate—not just accept without questioning—others' claims regarding the validity of a site, book, or other specific source of information. At this stage, one has to "make sense of information gathered from diverse sources by identifying misconceptions, main and supporting ideas, conflicting information, point of view, and biases" (American Association of School Librarians [AASL], 2009, p. 13) and conclude which sources/ information are valid and accurate by using conscious strategies rather than simply using intuitive judgments or "rules of thumb." This phase is the most challenging segment of health information seeking and serves as a determinant of success (or lack thereof) in the information-seeking process. The following section on Sources of Health Information further explains this phase.

The fifth phase is *information management*, whereby one has to organize information that has been gathered in some manner to ensure easy retrieval and use in the future. The last phase is *information use*, in which one will synthesize information found across various resources, draw conclusions, and locate the answer to his or her original question and/or the content that fulfills the information need. This phase also often involves implementation, such as using the information to solve a health problem; make health-related decisions; identify and engage in behaviors that will help a person to avoid health risks; share the health information found with family members and friends who may benefit from it; and advocate more broadly for personal, family, or community health.

THE IMPORTANCE OF HEALTH LITERACY

The conception of health has moved from a passive view (someone is either well or ill) to one that is more active and process based (someone is working toward preventing or managing disease). Hence, the dominant focus has shifted from doctors and treatments to patients and prevention, resulting in the need to strengthen our ability and confidence (as patients and consumers of health care) to look for, assess, understand, manage, share, adapt, and use health-related information. An individual's health literacy level has been found to predict his or her health status better than age, race, educational attainment, employment status, and income level (National Network of Libraries of Medicine, 2013). Greater health literacy also enables individuals to better communicate with health care providers such as doctors, nutritionists, and therapists, as they can pose more relevant, informed, and useful questions to health care providers. Another added advantage of greater health literacy is better information-seeking skills, not only for health but also in other domains, such as completing assignments for school.

SOURCES OF HEALTH INFORMATION: THE GOOD, THE BAD, AND THE IN-BETWEEN

For generations, doctors, nurses, nutritionists, health coaches, and other health professionals have been the trusted sources of health information. Additionally, researchers have found that young adults, when they have health-related questions, typically turn to a family member who has had firsthand experience with a health condition because of their family member's close proximity and because of their past experience with, and trust in, this individual. Expertise should be a core consideration when consulting a person, website, or book for health information. The credentials and background of the person or author and conflicting interests of the author (and his or her organization) must be checked and validated to ensure the likely credibility of the health information they are conveying. While books often have implied credibility because of the peer-review process involved, self-publishing has challenged this credibility, so qualifications of book authors should also be verified. When it comes to health information, currency of the source must also be examined. When examining health information/studies presented, pay attention to the exhaustiveness of research methods utilized to offer recommendations or conclusions. Small and nondiverse sample size is often—but not always—an indication of reduced credibility. Studies that confuse correlation with causation is another potential issue to watch for. Information seekers must also pay attention to the sponsors of the research studies. For example, if a study is sponsored by manufacturers of drug Y and the study recommends that drug Y is the best treatment to manage or cure a disease, this may indicate a lack of objectivity on the part of the researchers.

The Internet is rapidly becoming one of the main sources of health information. Online forums, news agencies, personal blogs, social media sites, pharmacy sites, and celebrity "doctors" are all offering medical and health information targeted to various types of people in regard to all types of diseases and symptoms. There are professional journalists, citizen journalists, hoaxers, and people paid to write fake health news on various sites that may appear to have a legitimate domain name and may even have authors who claim to have professional credentials, such as an MD. All these sites *may* offer useful information or information that appears to be useful and relevant; however, much of the information may be debatable and may fall into gray areas that require readers to discern credibility, reliability, and biases.

While broad recognition and acceptance of certain media, institutions, and people often serve as the most popular determining factors to assess credibility of health information among young people, keep in mind that there are legitimate Internet sites, databases, and books that publish health information and serve as sources of health information for doctors, other health sites, and members of the public. For example, MedlinePlus (https://medlineplus.gov) has trusted sources on over 975 diseases and conditions and presents the information in easy-to-understand language.

The chart here presents factors to consider when assessing credibility of health information. However, keep in mind that these factors function only as a guide and require continuous updating to keep abreast with the changes in the landscape of health information, information sources, and technologies.

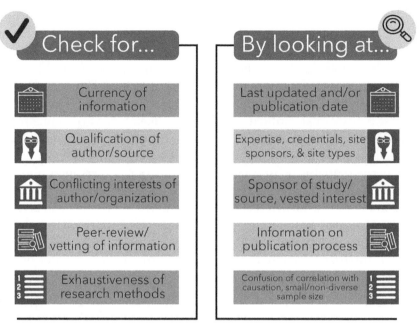

All images from flaticon.com

The chart can serve as a guide; however, approaching a librarian about how one can go about assessing the credibility of both print and online health information is far more effective than using generic checklist-type tools. While librarians are not health experts, they can apply and teach patrons strategies to determine the credibility of health information.

With the prevalence of fake sites and fake resources that appear to be legitimate, it is important to use the following health information assessment tips to verify health information that one has obtained (St. Jean et al., 2015, p. 151):

- **Don't assume you are right**: Even when you feel very sure about an answer, keep in mind that the answer may not be correct, and it is important to conduct (further) searches to validate the information.
- **Don't assume you are wrong**: You may actually have correct information, even if the information you encounter does not match—that is, you may be right and the resources that you have found may contain false information.
- **Take an open approach**: Maintain a critical stance by not including your preexisting beliefs as keywords (or letting them influence your choice of keywords) in a search, as this may influence what it is possible to find out.

- **Verify, verify, and verify**: Information found, especially on the Internet, needs to be validated, no matter how the information appears on the site (i.e., regardless of the appearance of the site or the quantity of information that is included).

Health literacy comes with experience navigating health information. Professional sources of health information, such as doctors, health care providers, and health databases, are still the best, but one also has the power to search for health information and then verify it by consulting with these trusted sources and by using the health information assessment tips and guide shared previously.

Mega Subramaniam, PhD
Associate Professor, College of Information
Studies, University of Maryland

REFERENCES AND FURTHER READING

American Association of School Librarians (AASL). (2009). *Standards for the 21st-century learner in action.* Chicago, IL: American Association of School Librarians.

Hilligoss, B., & Rieh, S.-Y. (2008). Developing a unifying framework of credibility assessment: Construct, heuristics, and interaction in context. *Information Processing & Management, 44*(4), 1467–1484.

Kuhlthau, C. C. (1988). Developing a model of the library search process: Cognitive and affective aspects. *Reference Quarterly, 28*(2), 232–242.

National Network of Libraries of Medicine (NNLM). (2013). Health literacy. Bethesda, MD: National Network of Libraries of Medicine. Retrieved from nnlm.gov/outreach/consumer/hlthlit.html

Ratzan, S. C., & Parker, R. M. (2000). Introduction. In C. R. Selden, M. Zorn, S. C. Ratzan, & R. M. Parker (Eds.), *National Library of Medicine current bibliographies in medicine: Health literacy.* NLM Pub. No. CBM 2000-1. Bethesda, MD: National Institutes of Health, U.S. Department of Health and Human Services.

St. Jean, B., Taylor, N. G., Kodama, C., & Subramaniam, M. (February 2017). Assessing the health information source perceptions of tweens using card-sorting exercises. *Journal of Information Science.* Retrieved from http://journals.sagepub.com/doi/abs/10.1177/0165551516687728

St. Jean, B., Subramaniam, M., Taylor, N. G., Follman, R., Kodama, C., & Casciotti, D. (2015). The influence of positive hypothesis testing on youths' online health-related information seeking. *New Library World, 116*(3/4), 136–154.

Subramaniam, M., St. Jean, B., Taylor, N. G., Kodama, C., Follman, R., & Casciotti, D. (2015). Bit by bit: Using design-based research to improve the health literacy of adolescents. *JMIR Research Protocols*, 4(2), paper e62. Retrieved from http://www.ncbi.nlm.nih.gov/pmc /articles/PMC4464334/

Valenza, J. (2016, November 26). Truth, truthiness, and triangulation: A news literacy toolkit for a "post-truth" world [Web log]. Retrieved from http://blogs.slj.com/neverendingsearch/2016/11/26/truth-truthi ness-triangulation-and-the-librarian-way-a-news-literacy-toolkit-for -a-post-truth-world/

Common Misconceptions about Grief and Loss

1. THERE IS A SPECIFIC WAY TO GRIEVE AND YOU MUST FOLLOW THE STAGES

Grief is often described as a process that happens in stages. However, grief does not happen in a fixed or ordered way and not everyone experiences every stage. Scholars and other experts in the field have noted typical responses when someone suffers a loss, but these reactions do not emerge for every person who is grieving or mourning. Grief can be cyclical, it can come and go, and is sometimes unpredictable. It involves a range of emotions and reactions. Questions 2 and 3 provide additional information about the stages of grief and other theories and models for understanding the process.

2. GRIEF TAKES ABOUT A YEAR

We may hear others say to those who are grieving that "it's been a year, it's time to get over it" or "time heals all wounds." Either comment reveals a misunderstanding of how loss is experienced. There is no standard or set time for grief. How one responds to loss takes its own course, and the grieving process is unique to each person regarding how it occurs and the time it may take. Some even insist that grief never ends, and instead changes over time. Question 21 addresses this topic in more detail.

3. GRIEF IS SOMETHING WE MUST BEAR ALONE

A person suffering loss will deal with intense feelings that are deeply personal and unique. They are often scary and overwhelming, and the grieving person may feel self-conscious or embarrassed to share such emotions. However, many of the ways we experience healthy grief involve things like telling stories, embracing memories, or engaging in relationships that offer empathy and support. Sharing feelings with trusted friends, family, loved ones, fellow students, counselors, or a mental health professional combats loneliness, isolation, or other harmful emotions that subvert progress toward health and healing. Questions 30–37 offer guidance on seeking and offering support during the grieving process.

4. GRIEF IS EXPERIENCED ONLY WHEN SOMEONE IMPORTANT TO YOU DIES

Grief is a response to loss. Although the death of a loved one or friend are primary losses, there are many other types, both large and small, that can lead to grief and mourning. Questions 16–20 focus on nondeath sources of grief, including divorce, sexual assault, bullying, and breakups.

5. GRIEF AND LOSS AFFECT ADULTS, CHILDREN, AND YOUTH IN THE SAME WAY

Parents or adults may expect their teenager or young adult to respond to loss in ways similar to their own. However, cognitive, emotional, social, psychological, and spiritual development and experience differ by individual and change as we age. Consequently, loss will be framed in ways distinct or unique to a particular stage in life. Understanding these differences allows grief to happen in more constructive ways and helps adults empathize with and better care for young people experiencing the trauma of loss. This topic is covered in more detail in Question 6.

QUESTIONS AND ANSWERS

❖❖❖

The Basics

1. What is grief?

Emma loses a pair of earrings given to her by her grandmother for her eighteenth birthday. A family heirloom, the earrings were deeply cherished and Emma is downhearted for weeks.

Josh's family moves to another state before his junior year. He struggles in the first few months in the new high school.

Liam's favorite uncle is killed in a car accident. He and his family are overcome by shock and sorrow.

Madison is turned down at her first and second choice for college. Though she is accepted to three other schools, she can't help feeling sad.

Loss can happen in many ways in our life. Grief, simply put, is the reaction or response to loss. But, it may be difficult to know what to expect or how to react when loss occurs, especially life-changing losses. You've probably heard various thoughts about grief and many of them negative. "You should be over this by now." "Don't cry so much." "If you're losing sleep, well that's just not normal." "What do you mean you can't believe they're gone?" "It was just a job." "You'll find another boyfriend." Friends may avoid you if you're in mourning or sad for too long, or parents might pressure you to get it together. Death and loss are hard to talk about and deal with. It's as if grieving is to be avoided or limited, or that certain ways of grieving are abnormal.

However, grief is a natural response. Though it may feel overwhelming at first, healthy grief is not unending and usually helps us cope with the loss, adapt to new ways of relating to others, and leads us to explore different approaches to life or adopt new habits or traditions. Of course, some who are bereaved may become overwhelmed for longer periods by sadness or chronic grief. These situations need extra care and attention. However, even in such cases, healing and a renewed outlook are possible and expected.

Grief is also a universal experience that can be described in ways that sound familiar to anyone who has grieved or mourned. *A Grief Observed,* C.S. Lewis's 1961 book about his struggles with the death of his wife, begins this way, "No one ever told me that grief felt so like fear. I am not afraid, but the sensation is like being afraid. The same fluttering in the stomach, the same restlessness, the yawning. I keep swallowing." For anyone who has experienced the death of someone, or the loss of something significant, these sensations will probably feel recognizable.

Yet, grief is not one or two dimensional or just an emotional reaction. It touches on physical, emotional, spiritual, social, and psychological responses to loss. It affects other aspects of our life too, including philosophical and cultural issues or the way we think about the world. The intensity of grief and the direction it takes may differ for more serious losses, but the pain we feel, or the despair that arises, is no less important whatever the loss may be.

Bereavement experts have outlined numerous reactions that are part of the normal grieving process. These include expected feelings and reactions like shock, sadness, crying, anger, or mild depression. The bereaved person may experience physical maladies like stomach issues or sleep disturbances. Other common responses include feelings of guilt, preoccupation with the loss, anxiety, problems with eating, despair, fear, or loneliness. Positive emotions also arise when dealing with loss. For example, relief may be experienced after someone with a long, difficult illness had died. Or, laughter often erupts when friends or family share humorous stories and memories about a loved one they've lost.

Despite the fact there are recognizable patterns to grief and mourning, these patterns and similarities are not static and predictable. The way grief is experienced is unique to each person as Lewis discovered and shares in his account of grief: "I thought I could describe [grief as] a *state*; make a map of sorrow. Sorrow, however, turns out not to be a state but a process. It needs not a map but a history. . . ." Moreover, the timing of the grieving process is different for each person. The manner and timing of the grief process are dependent on a number of factors, including the closeness of the person, the importance of a job or special possession, circumstances around the loss or death, how one copes with crises or life circumstances, and the access to support persons or systems.

More will be said in the following questions about this process and history, including thoughts about normal and healthy grief, types of grief, ways to help or find assistance, a few insights regarding misconceptions of grief, and problematic or chronic grief.

2. I've heard about the stages of grief. What are they?

Even if someone knows little else about bereavement they have probably heard of the stages of grief. The stages became popularized in the early seventies after the 1969 publication of Elisabeth Kübler-Ross's book *On Death and Dying*. In it, Kübler-Ross described five stages a dying person goes through as they face the reality of their impending death. These descriptions also became known as stages of grief and were applied to the process that a bereaved person goes through as they deal with loss. The book was written after interviews with numerous patients who were dying and helped bring light to end-of-life issues, a subject too long ignored by the medical community. It was also written to serve as a guide to family members, as well as clergy, nurses, and doctors who were working with the dying.

The five stages that Kübler-Ross identified were denial, anger, bargaining, depression, and acceptance. Simply stated, *denial* involved the patient questioning the truth of the diagnosis and preferring or imagining an alternative version of circumstances that excluded acceptance of a terminal illness. *Anger* was the next stage and encompassed questions like "Why me?" and feelings of rage, resentment, bitterness, and hostility. Anger could be directed toward doctors and health care workers, family members and friends, God, the universe, or even focused inward. *Bargaining* was the third stage and involved things like negotiating with a higher power, or rationalizing ways to escape the prognosis, or seeking a change in lifestyle as a way to bargain for more time or a reverse of circumstances. Becoming resigned to the prognosis led to the next stage, *depression*, and feelings of hopelessness and despair. In this stage, the person could become distant and lose heart, and fail to find comfort in relationships or engaging in everyday life. In the fifth and last stage, *acceptance*, the dying person embraces the reality of the terminal illness, becomes reflective and begins to ready themselves, and even their loved ones, for the inevitable future. This stage might involve healing relationships, dealing with issues that offer care for the family, and a sense of peace. At times, the person who is dying reaches this stage before those who will be grieving their loss.

However, Kübler-Ross was not the first to speak of stages, or to describe the work a person needed to accomplish as they grieve. Sigmund Freud is credited with the notion of grief work, though his examination of grief and mourning did not mention stages or tasks. His ideas about grief and mourning were shared in a 1917 paper entitled "Mourning and Melancholia," which compared grief responses with depression. However, the work was more speculative in nature and not based in research.

In 1944, Erich Lindemann published a landmark work exploring grief and mourning. It was a study based on interviews with bereaved families and survivors of the Cocoanut Grove nightclub fire of 1942 that killed nearly 500 people. In his paper, Lindemann noted five characteristics of the bereaved and argued that necessary grief work needed to be done in order to find health and healing. He also claimed positive emotional reactions to loss might be problematic, especially if experienced too soon, or without doing the necessary work. Suppressing feelings and failing to properly face the tasks of grief could lead, in his opinion, to unresolved grief and later psychological issues. As with Freud, though, his conclusions were untested by necessary long-term research based in reliable measurements.

Since Kübler-Ross's work, numerous books and articles written about grief and loss refer to her categories, or rework and add stages to offer a deeper and richer account of the experience of the dying person. In *Good Grief*, Granger E. Westberg's short, yet classic book, there are ten stages listed which include shock, depression, guilt, physical symptoms of distress, and hope.

Even though reference to stages has dominated the way healthy grief work has been described, it is a notion often criticized by those who study bereavement or deal with those who are grieving. Even the authors who describe the grief process in terms of stages have acknowledged difficulties, but still adhere to stages as a good way to illustrate patterns and work the bereaved person will face. One of the issues with Kübler-Ross's framework is that her examination is based on interviews with dying patients rather than with those who are grieving the loss of a loved one. Though there are insights regarding loss that are common to both populations, the experiences of the dying are of a different quality and direction than those who suffer loss.

There are other problems as well regarding the Kübler-Ross model or Lindemann's findings. The stages described by both are too limiting regarding the breadth of experience for those who grieve and do not take into full account other aspects of life like cultural, psychological, or spiritual influences. Though their reflections are based on numerous interviews, there is no subsequent research that indicates bereaved persons experience the stages in some linear or predictable pattern, or that the process of grief can be described by stages. Many of the bereaved may go through things like anger and depression, but not everyone who grieves deals with all the issues described by Kübler-Ross and Lindemann, or other authors who name stages. Other bereavement specialists suggest there is and has been too much of a reliance on stage theory. Some are also critical of the belief that the bereaved must go through stages in order to complete the necessary work of grief, or that the early stages of grief must avoid positive emotional reactions.

Even though there are valid criticisms of stage theory, Kübler-Ross and others addressed issues that had been ignored by medical, psychological, and spiritual professionals. Their pioneering work eventually led to further research and study around grief and loss, becoming a discipline that has grown into a more thorough, evidenced-based exploration of the phenomenon of bereavement, grief, and mourning.

3. Are there newer models and theories for understanding grief?

In light of criticisms about stages of grief, as well as a move to provide evidence-based research and study regarding bereavement, other theories and models have emerged to describe the grief process. A brief description of some of these ideas follows as a way to acknowledge and illustrate the various ways grief and mourning are understood.

Attachment theory has become one of the ways to conceptualize a person's reaction to loss. The theory was developed initially by John Bowlby, a British doctor and psychoanalyst, and arose from Bowlby's study of children and their caregivers. It concerns the importance of the principal attachment of an infant or child with their mother or a primary caregiver. The theory expanded to include the notion that the quality of this attachment not only affected the child's immediate relationships but could also affect relationships later in life. The model also explained that the primary attachment, as well as subsequent important relationships, are forged for particular reasons: safety, developing basic trust, having a secure foundation from which to explore the world, healthy development of identity and moral behavior, and as a defense against trauma. Bowlby also observed that infants or children separated from the person of primary attachment go through a series of reactions (or stages) like protest, anger, sadness, despair, withdrawal, and disorganization. All of these issues are of importance when considering the process of grief.

A number of theories and models regarding bereavement and grief reactions based on attachment theory have arisen. For example, some suggest that the strength and direction of the reaction to loss and the depth of the grief will be influenced by the depth and breadth of the attachment to the person who has died, or the job lost, or the friends left behind after a move. These models based on the patterns of attachment (see Glossary) are used by those providing care to grieving persons, especially those dealing with chronic or complicated grief (see Question 27).

Another development regarding the grief response is the use of categories like tasks instead of stages. *Tasks of grieving or mourning* focus on prescriptive rather than descriptive accounts and are attentive to what the grieving person needs to do or accomplish through the grief process rather than describing thoughts, reactions, and behaviors. There are several authors and practitioners who emphasize tasks as critical for the grief process. For example, in the fifth edition of J. William Worden's *Grief Counseling and Grief Therapy: A Handbook for the Mental Health Practitioner*, he suggests four "tasks of mourning" as a way to understand the grief process. For him, addressing each task is critical for coping effectively with the loss. The first task involves *accepting the reality of the loss* and includes dealing with the various forms of denial that often accompany loss. Intellectual and emotional acceptance is essential for completing this task. The second task seeks to *process the pain of grief*. This category involves facing emotional pain as well as physical pain and aberrant behavior. Pain can be from sadness or anger, as well as other emotional responses. Worden believes ignoring or suppressing the pain can affect the length of time needed to mourn or lead to deeper emotional or medical issues. The third task entails *adjusting to a world without the deceased*. In this task the bereaved seeks to learn how to function differently in the world (external adjustment), come to a different or greater understanding of self (internal adjustment), and confront values, life direction, beliefs, and how one sees or views the world or a higher power (spiritual adjustment). Worden concludes with the fourth task, which focuses on *how to remember the deceased* while still going on with life. This task acknowledges that earlier ideas about the grief process, namely that the bereaved need to emotionally and psychologically separate from the deceased (Freud's belief), can actually harm the mourner's well-being. Instead, keeping a connection is critical for healing. Worden comments that this is often the most difficult task to complete, since many who are mourning may get stuck in their grief.

Another approach to grief and mourning developed by Terry L. Martin and Kenneth J. Doka describes grieving styles. Their model recognizes that grieving is complex and unique for each person and is affected by things like culture and personality. Martin and Doka identify three particular styles: *instrumental, intuitive,* and *blended* grief. In basic terms, they suggest that some deal with loss through feelings and process grief through conversation, support networks, and therapy (intuitive). Other bereaved persons take a more cognitive approach and may process through completing tasks or problem-solving. These individuals are more apt to control their feelings (instrumental). Those who experience blended grieving utilize both styles, though one may be dominant. Martin and Doka also suggest that problems can arise when a person mourns in a way contrary to their natural grieving style. For example, cultural stereotypes may deprive the bereaved from a healthy grief process. A female who processes instrumentally may feel pressure to show more emotion or talk about her feelings. An intuitive male could be criticized for being overemotional and told to "get it together."

The *dual process model* is yet another emergent concept to describe how grief happens. Developed by Margaret Stroebe, Henk Schut, and others, it describes two types of stressors that can affect bereavement: *loss* stressors and *restoration* stressors. The former stressor involves the emotions, thoughts, and actions surrounding the actual loss or death. The latter focuses more on life changes and secondary losses that occur as the bereaved adapt to the loss. A key aspect of this model is *oscillation.* As the bereaved copes with the loss, they will move back and forth between the two stressors. They can also move between confronting and avoiding the stresses and changes that accompany loss and adaption.

There are a number of other models like Therese Rando's *Six "R" Model of Mourning,* which focuses on the six needs of the mourner, and *Constructivism,* which deals with the need for the bereaved to make sense of the experiences surrounding grief and create new meaning in their lives.

George Bonanno, a professor in clinical psychology, who has done extensive research regarding bereavement, takes a slightly different approach. He rejects the notion that grief work needs to be done by those who suffer loss, or that the bereaved, on the whole, actually go through stages or need to complete tasks to return to health or move on with their life. His 2009 book, *The Other Side of Sadness,* describes common patterns of grief which focus on how one adapts to the loss. Some who experience loss suffer *chronic* grief, which means the bereaved are over-whelmed by their loss and find it difficult to return to some normalcy or make new meaning. Chronic grief can last for years. *Recovery* is another pattern in which the person who suffers loss experiences difficulties while mourning, sometimes acutely, but eventually moves toward healing and a meaningful life. However, Bonanno suggests that the majority of those who experience loss are *resilient*, suffering relatively minor disruptions in their life and can simply move on and do what needs to be done after a death or loss (see Question 36). Though one may experience shock or feel pain intensely because of loss, he indicates bereavement "is a human experience. It is something we are wired for, and it is certainly not meant to overwhelm us." Bonanno also echoes the work of Stroebe and Schut but suggests the extent of fluctuation in emotional response and well-being that occur as a person grieves is more pronounced than indicated in their research. By emphasizing that response to loss is indeed more wave-like in nature, he seeks to dispel the notion that grief happens in stages or phases.

Most of the research and models mentioned focus on adult subjects. Although the research may lead to theories and reasonable ideas con-cerning how children, youth, and young adults grieve and mourn, there are not enough evidence-based studies to make definitive claims. In other words, grief research is ongoing and much is being learned about how human beings of all ages and backgrounds react and respond to loss. How-ever, the various models and descriptions of the grieving process speak clearly to the depth and complexity of bereavement. What is emerging from bereavement research is a consensus that response to loss is unique for each person and is dependent on a number of factors and circum-stances. When dealing with grief, then, it is important to consider the various models and possible responses and cease to limit our understand-ing to a particular viewpoint or popular theory.

4. What's the difference between grief, mourning, and bereavement?

The words grief, mourning, and bereavement are often used interchange-ably, which is not surprising since all denote aspects of loss or the response to loss. It's helpful, then, to get a sense of what these terms mean and how they are related to one another.

Bereavement is the easiest of the terms to define. It simply refers to the state of loss, or the experience of having lost someone close or something important. Bereavement does not describe the process or response. When a person is said to be bereaved, it simply means they have suffered a loss. Bereavement research or literature describes studies and resources focused on loss.

Grief, as already discussed, refers to a person's reaction or response to loss. Grief typically describes the internal reactions and are more than just emotional ones. They can involve thoughts as well as particular behaviors and physical responses. Grief reactions are often tied to cultural, social, or spiritual norms or values for the bereaved person.

Mourning also refers to a person or group's reaction but is usually focused on the external behaviors and actions. So, if grief describes the internal experience and response to loss, mourning is thought to be the external or public expression of the internal feelings and thoughts. For example, a funeral or memorial service is a way in which loved ones and friends mourn the death of a relative or friend. It is through the funeral that public expression is given to the internal pain or sadness or shock surrounding the loss as well as an avenue for hope and healing. Mourning in different cultures may involve particular customs that have evolved to deal with death and loss (see Question 39).

If grief is more internal, it may be difficult to notice whether a person is grieving or not. Although crying or physical pain or sleeplessness are part of the grieving process and typically more visible, the bereaved person may hide these responses from close friends and family. It may be difficult to tell how sad someone might be, or the loneliness they experience, or the guilt they may be feeling. However, some aspects of mourning allow the bereaved a chance to express or acknowledge feelings within. The mourner may recognize they are not alone in their grief. When friends light a candle or create a memorial at the roadside of a tragic accident, they are involved in mourning, and hopefully in working through mutual feelings associated with grief. When a daughter creates a new picture mural for her wall after the divorce of her parents, it can be an outward expression of her struggles with internal emotions and thoughts, or may signify an important step in her acceptance and adjustment to a new way of life.

Although the definitions and differences between grief and mourning can be described in these ways, there are other definitions that are important. In the fifth edition of his book *Grief Counseling and Grief Therapy*, J. William Worden offers a slightly different view of grief and mourning. Worden uses the term grief "to indicate the *experience* of one who has lost a loved one to death. It is comprised of thoughts, feelings, behaviors, and psychological changes that vary in pattern and intensity over time." For him, there are some behaviors that are usually associated with mourning that he includes with grief, like visiting sites that remind the bereaved person of their loved one who has died. However, most of what he considers grief is consistent with how other bereavement professionals conceptualize the term.

Mourning, he says, "is the term applied to the *process* that one goes through in *adapting* to the death of the person. The finality and consequences of the loss are understood and assimilated into the life of the mourner." The process he mentions includes tasks that he believes each bereaved person encounters as they cope with loss. So, when some speak of stages of grief, or the tasks of grief, or the process of grief, Worden would consider these the stages or tasks of mourning (see Question 3).

Since there is some disagreement among the experts, and a few behaviors can easily be considered part of grief or mourning, it may be difficult to give an absolute definition for these terms. However, the ambiguity should not seriously affect discussion and discovery about the various aspects of loss and how it affects our lives. For this volume, though, grief will be the more encompassing term. It will be used to describe the internal process and stages, which will include feelings, thoughts, values, spirituality, and even a few behaviors. Mourning will be focused more on the "public expression" of grief and will address the cultural and social aspects of responses to loss. Of course, overlap will happen and hopefully will not confuse or diminish the discussion.

5. What's the difference between grief and depression?

This question is challenging to answer because aspects of grief can look like manifestations of depression. Moreover, some of the classic descriptions of the process of grief include depression as a stage or typical response. However, depression and grief are distinct conditions and care should be given to recognize what they are and how they are conceived. Though important to distinguish the two, understanding the close link between grief and depression is also crucial. Signs of a more serious form of grief, namely complicated grief, also overlap with symptoms of depression and post-traumatic stress disorder (PTSD). Those associations and disparities will be addressed in Question 27.

Grief is a response to loss and it can be expressed in many ways (see Questions 2 and 3). It includes emotional, psychological, behavioral, spiritual, physical and social responses that can affect, and be affected by other beliefs, attitudes and cultural values. Though bereaved persons often exhibit typical responses (e.g., sadness, shock, crying, anger, adapting to the loss), grief cannot be described as having definitive patterns or stages of behavior since the reaction to loss is unique for each person. Definitions for mental disorders, like depression, describe agreed upon mental or behavioral patterns that disrupt normal functioning. Though mental disorders can involve a singular episode, they are often persistent and diagnosis may require that a pattern of behavior or thinking be manifested over a certain period of time. For example, diagnosis of major depressive disorder requires that a particular set of criteria be met over a two-week period at least and is distinct from mild depression (see Glossary).

It's not difficult, though, to see the connection between grief and depression. Sadness, which is a typical reaction of bereaved people, is also a characteristic feeling for those with depression. Grief and depression exhibit other common feelings and behaviors such as anger, guilt, episodes of crying, anxiety, fear and despair. A bereaved teenager may have trouble concentrating, may miss school or fail to turn in schoolwork, lose sleep, will sometimes avoid friends and family, and may become involved in risky behaviors. Likewise, a young person suffering from depression may exhibit these same actions, yet in a more intense way. Mild depression is sometimes observed in those who are grieving and is thought to be a normal part of the process. However, persistent and more acute emotions and behaviors may be a sign of major depression that will likely require the help of a psychologist or therapist. Major depression also inhibits normal coping and problem-solving abilities and will likely complicate grief responses.

Discerning the difference between feelings and behaviors that are a normal part of grief from those that are characteristic of mild depression (or adjustment disorder) or major depression (or major depression disorder) is important. The following are some of the ways to distinguish symptoms of normal grief from those that typify serious forms of depression.

- Typically, a bereaved person will recognize symptoms of depression as a normal part of grief. Those who are exhibiting normal grief responses like deep sadness and anger will also be able to laugh and have positive feelings about the deceased. They may experience relief if the death was the result of a long-term illness. The person suffering more acute forms of depression will struggle to see beyond the depressive feelings and will not be able to experience positive feelings about the deceased, themselves, or the world. Instead of possible feelings of relief after a prolonged or difficult death, the young person suffering major depression may feel increasing distress and burden.

- Normal grief responses are usually episodic, oscillating, or wave like (see Question 3). For teenagers and young adults who exhibit typical grief responses, their internal compass will help them focus on the feelings that accompany grief at various times, and then take an emotional and mental break when needed. On the other hand, major depression involves negative feelings and reactions that become prolonged and persistent. Young people suffering deeper depression will often be unaware of warning signs or consequences of their actions.

- Grief and mourning are typically focused on the deceased, the manner of death, worries about the family or future, and even guilt associated with the death or relationship with the deceased. Depression usually involves a preoccupation with low self-esteem, persistent withdrawal from family, friends and activities, as well a pervasive and general sense of guilt and shame that has little to do with the deceased.

- Those teenagers and young adults who are grieving in fairly normal ways do not usually have thoughts of suicide, nor do they attempt suicide. One of the signs of major depression or major depressive disorder are constant thoughts of the young person about suicide or death.

- The bereaved teenager and young adult will miss the friend or loved one that has died and will feel as though the wonder of the world is diminished without them. Even so, the bereaved can work to find ways to seek hope and healing, oftentimes inspired by the life of their loved one or friend. A person suffering from depression sees no light in the world; they may feel the world around them and within them is inherently deficient or dysfunctional. A seriously depressed young person may also feel worthless and negative about the world and themselves.

In summary, those who are supporting grieving teenagers and young adults will see bouts of sadness or even mild depression. But the bereaved will also show positive signs, will be able to bounce back, and may actively work toward coping with and healing from the loss. On the other hand, those suffering from depression for periods that cause concern include the following feelings, behaviors, and thoughts: hopelessness, suicidal thoughts or attempts, desperation, pervasive loss of interest or pleasure in normal activities, persistent use (and abuse) of alcohol or recreational drugs, noticeable problems dealing with daily activities, feelings of worthlessness, frequent thoughts about death, slowed thinking, speaking or body movements, and withdrawal from others and life activities and events. Again, some of these responses can be witnessed in normal grieving patterns, like the abuse of alcohol and drugs, or loss of interest in normal daily activities, but with typical grief and mourning, these reactions are not prolonged and usually become less persistent and intense.

The remedies for coping with uncomplicated or normal grief are also quite different than that for treating major depression. For the typical grief process, helping the bereaved young person identify and express feelings is usually helpful, as is finding meaning in the loss, dealing with living without the deceased and finding ways to remember their friend or loved one who has died. There are a variety of ways for those grieving to find healing and new meaning (see especially Questions 30–37). Many times, having the right support group of friends, family, teachers, counselors, or online resources are enough for the bereaved young person to find the help needed. Depression, on the other hand, is treated through psychotherapy and medication. The scope and description of various psychotherapies will not be included here, but they deal more intensely with feelings, history, connections, possible issues of abuse, and digging deeper into other associated issues or disorders (like major anxiety, multiple major losses occurring at the same time, or sexual assault).

Whenever a young person is grieving, it is important for them to stay connected to trusted family and friends who can support and stay attentive to the bereaved person's moods and reactions. If necessary, it is also essential to connect the bereaved teenager or young adult with mental health and bereavement professionals if their grief responses are prolonged and become more intense over time. Determining the extent of depression should be dealt with by a mental health practitioner and/or bereavement specialist.

6. How does a person's age impact their grieving process?

Ample studies have been done around developmental stages from infant to adult. For example, Erik and Joan Erickson's theories around psychological development are well known; they conceived eight stages of development that encompassed psychological, biological, and social factors. Usually, developmental theories also involve particular tasks associated with each phase. Those who work with and study grief among children and youth have noticed that age and psychological development impacts bereavement. Dealing with grief and loss can also affect psychological and emotional development.

Bereavement characteristics of children and youth are often categorized by chronological age, since developmental age or stages typically parallel chronological age. However, the categories are guidelines and certainly not exact, and a young person's chronological age and developmental stage may not progress in typical patterns. Atypical behavior can also arise when a teenager or young adult suffers the trauma of loss. For example, there are times when a teenager (or young adult) may exhibit traits in bereavement similar to older children (like magical thinking, acting out), while a young person may also respond to grief in ways typical of older adults. Even though developmental stages are important, there are a number of other factors that affect bereavement for teenagers and young adults, like their relationship to the person who died, family dynamics, or how responses to grief, crisis, and trauma have been modeled by parents or other close adults. Whatever the developmental age or reactions may be, the grief experienced by teenagers and young adults is usually far more complex and nuanced that older adults assume.

There are a number of developmental tasks that come to mind when considering a young person's response to grief and loss. For instance, teenage and young adult years often revolve around the young person becoming independent, developing lasting relationships different from family, and moving toward vocational thoughts and pursuits. Struggles around independence and wanting to spend time with peers is tested by significant loss, especially related to the death of a family member of close family friend. There can be a conflict between needing to separate from parents and the desire to be more helpful at home. The death of a family member, and the circumstances and grief that arise, may contribute to the bereaved young person feeling different from peers, which can sometimes lead to a sense of isolation. A significant death in the family may also have an effect on future plans and vocational aspirations.

Other matters of concern as the teenager evolves and deals with the multiple changes occurring in their life (e.g., physical, emotional, psychological) are issues around fairness and justice in the world, developing self-confidence, figuring out how to manage life and gaining life-skills, dealing with a need to fit in, seeking meaning and purpose, and trusting in the predictability of events. Coping with grief can touch on all of these concerns. In fact, experiencing a significant loss can have a profound impact on attention to these and other tasks and the ability of young people to transition through adolescence to adulthood. Such feelings and difficulties are not exclusive to young people, as adults may also be hindered regarding development and embracing change.

Although grief reactions may vary for individuals, there are typical responses and behaviors consistent with teenagers and young adults that are associated with developmental stages. It's often the case that young people thirteen to eighteen years old may become more withdrawn after a significant loss, unsure whether friends can identify, and find it difficult to share with parents. Young people may feel uncertain about their role within the family or may take on responsibilities of adults around them, especially if the older adults are struggling with their own grief. There are often feelings of guilt, especially if the relationship with the person who died was strained, or the young person may feel their behavior somehow caused the illness or tragic event that led to the death. Teenagers and young adults typically want to be involved in funeral arrangements or decisions that need to be made for the family (or themselves), and become understandably resentful if left out. Because there are so many changes in feelings, thoughts, physical attributes, meaning, and spirituality at this point in life, the extra burden of loss may lead to intense feelings of anger or sadness. Sometimes young people will skip school or their academic performance may decline. Teenagers and young adults may seek to cope by engaging in risky behavior (e.g., taking drugs, abusing alcohol, sexual activity), which may temporarily ease the pain or release tension but is harmful to long-term health and well-being.

Similar responses may occur for young adults, though their grief reactions may be more like older adults. There are also differences for older teenagers and those in their early twenties who have started careers or who have children. They may deal with losses that younger teenagers typically do not deal with—like the loss of a child, abortion, the loss of a livelihood while supporting a family, and the loss of a dream around college or a career (see Questions 11 and 20).

Those who work with bereaved teenagers and young adults suggest coping strategies that are more suitable in light of developmental concerns of young people in the midst of grief. For example, a thirteen-year-old does not want to be treated like a child when dealing with death, just as an eighteen-year-old would be frustrated by being left out of decisions that may affect their future. Young people of all ages seek honesty and openness around issues that arise in bereavement and to be treated with respect. Allowing the young person space for their own beliefs and understandings, even when different from the family, is also important, as is being part of planning for the funeral or decisions about the next place to live. It's also critical to offer teenagers choices instead of making demands and to be sensitive to fluctuations in feelings. Although a young person may be asserting independence, it does not mean they have "moved on." Patience and thoughtful care are necessary as the young person sorts out needs and beliefs. As with older adults, teenagers and young adults need assurance, especially regarding safety, security, and love. Exercise, healthy habits, play, and chances to spend time in solitude are also essential aspects of a healthy grief process. It's important for young people to be connected to a support system, even if it is outside the family. Another trusted adult, a peer support group, or other helpful resources (like grief/ bereavement professionals, websites oriented toward grief support) are to be encouraged. Young people also benefit from parents or other adults who model appropriate expressions of grief and self-care.

How Will Grief Be Different . . .

7. . . . with the death of a sibling?

One of the most difficult experiences of loss is the death of a sibling—it is a profound life-changing experience. There are many issues that arise when someone loses a brother or sister and the depth of loss is sometimes unacknowledged. Such grief can be more challenging because of other relationships involved. The loss of a child is significant and heart-wrenching for parents, and their grief is typically the object of focused care and concern. The parents also may become excessively preoccupied with the death. When this happens, the needs of siblings and other family members may be overlooked or even discounted. A surviving brother or sister may be asked to "stay strong" for the sake of their parents; they may even be afraid to upset their parents. At times, the sibling(s) may be the one(s) offering daily comfort for their mother and/or father, giving them space to grieve while their needs go relatively unmet. A prime example can be found in A Christmas Carol, the classic novella by Charles Dickens. In one passage, the Ghost of Christmas Yet to Come shows Ebenezer Scrooge a scene depicting Bob Cratchit's family mourning the loss of Tiny Tim. In the passage, Bob Cratchit's grief receives the most attention, with some of Tiny Tim's siblings offering comfort to their father.

The intensity of grief will also depend on issues like the depth of relationship (attachment) with the deceased sibling, the proximity of age,
the number of siblings in a family (and the strength of family bonds),
if the deceased sibling had moved away, the relationship of the parents
with the deceased sibling, if the deceased is a stepbrother/stepsister, how
the sibling died and other factors.

Oftentimes the sibling is a peer and deep feelings of kinship are involved.
The surviving brother or sister may feel like they've lost a friend, or someone close they can talk with and trust. The closer in age the siblings, the
deeper the trauma and threat to the survivor's identity. There may even
be a greater fear of death. Those who work with bereaved siblings also
notice heightened feelings of guilt and self-blame, especially if the surviving sibling was somehow involved (for example, in an accident) or close
by when the brother or sister died. Guilt or regret can also arise if there
had been a recent argument with the brother or sister, or if the surviving
sibling was insensitive or critical of the sibling who died.

When there are two or more bereaved siblings, the relationship(s)
between the surviving brothers and sisters can become strained or, con-
versely, may serve as a source of support. The way the siblings handle
the trauma can depend on the ages of the other siblings, the relationships they have with the parents and each other, as well as the role they
play in the family—or the role they are expected to take on after the
death of their loved one. If the parents are overwhelmed by grief, then
the more difficult it will be for the children to adapt and adjust, unless an
older teenager or young adult sibling offers needed care and acts as a role
model. If the surviving youth is now an "only child," there is the potential
for substantial change in roles and relationships. Sometimes the parents
may unconsciously expect the surviving child to take on the role of their
deceased sibling.

Other typical grief reactions can be present and amplified. As with
other deaths, the bereaved youth may become isolated, feeling that their
peers, teachers, parents, and other adults simply cannot understand their
loss. Bereavement experts also note that those who lose siblings feel a
heightened sense of vulnerability and loss of security and are at a greater
risk of anxiety, depression and other mental challenges in adulthood.

Parents and other adults will often deny information about the death,
which can complicate grief and prevent the necessary narrative needed
by the surviving sibling to cope with the loss. As in other losses of loved
ones, there will often be a need to be involved in the funeral or memorial
service as well as family conversations about the future.

The ability to cope in healthy ways with the death of a sibling is often tied to the response of the parents and the ability of the family unit as a whole to face the death together. Healthy grief can emerge when there is an openness to difficult conversations about fears, concerns, and the depth of loss, or when the family can share about resentments, anger, or other feelings that may emerge. The ability to tell stories about the deceased brother and sister, and to remember them in meaningful ways, also contributes to the ability to cope and adapt to the new circumstances and relationships that will emerge. Encouraging surviving siblings to explore identity honestly amidst changing roles and family dynamics is also critical.

A sense of being loved and cared for is important for anyone facing traumatic loss, but is especially true for surviving siblings. Bereavement experts suggest, again, that the ability of the parents to cope with the loss is critical and central for the surviving children as they grieve and mourn. However, if the parents are unable to offer support because of their own struggles with grief, the attention and care of other significant adults or the support and presence of other siblings and friends, and having someone listen to the pain, are essential as one grieves the loss of a sister or brother.

8. . . . with the death of a parent?

The death of anyone close is a traumatic event in the life of a teen or young adult. The death of a parent, though, can be particularly devastating and the grief process can feel overwhelming. The reactions that occur when a parent dies is influenced by a number of factors. The strength of the bonds the child had with their deceased parent will potentially affect the grieving process. If a teenager and parent had a strong and healthy relationship it will certainly make the loss feel deeper and potentially difficult to deal with. However, strong relational connections often nurture an inner strength and confident outlook in the young person which could help them better navigate the grieving process.

If the relationship was strained, or some other dysfunction arose in the parent/child relationship or in the family system, then grief could take a variety of paths. A youth might feel relief, and then guilty for such feelings after their parent dies. Or guilt could arise if the teen felt the death was somehow their fault, or because they failed to help resolve conflicts and problems. There may be regret that resolution of the problems will not be possible, which could undermine a sense of hope or affect how long grief might last. Perhaps, the deceased parent was dealing with other issues like drug or alcohol addiction, or was physically or emotionally abusive. In these situations, the bereaved youth could encounter more complicated grief (see Question 27).

The role that the deceased parent had in the family system (bread-winner, nurturer, caretaker, disciplinarian, organizer) is also important. If the role was significant and impacted much of the way the family worked together or engaged life, then the disruption caused might affect the teen's ability to cope. Greater instability could undermine a sense of control, or even deeply held spiritual values. At times, the teen/young adult may feel drawn to take on one of the roles of the parent that died in an attempt to regain control or provide stability. Or they may be expected to fill the role of the deceased parent, especially if the surviving parent is having difficulty coping or is acting out in dysfunctional ways.

As the young person grieves the loss of their parent, they may encounter feelings around the future absence of their mother or father. Major events like graduation, marriage, job promotions, or having children will be affected and grief may emerge again around important occasions and milestones. Often, the young person who loses a parent feels different than their peers, and though friends are an important support when someone is grieving, the teen may feel their friends will be unable to relate and help. Anger, depression, and withdrawal are possible reactions too. The intensity and length of these and other grief responses will be unique to each young person, even siblings within the same family.

No matter the relationship with the parent, the young person will likely deal with issues around stability and security. Financial issues for the family may become a sudden concern. Daily routines and expectations will be disrupted. Young adults in college may wonder if they can or should stay in school. If the parent that dies is the mother, emotional setbacks may be more common. So, when a young person experiences the death of a parent, particular needs typically surface. Some of those needs include the ability to talk openly about the deceased parent, being nurtured and cared for, maintaining close relationships with friends, and staying on top of studies including plans for future school or employment. The death of a parent certainly disrupts these needs, and careful attention should be given to these life concerns. The way in which these needs are addressed certainly impact the grief process as well. Decision-making power is important as the youth looks to their future.

Often, youth are left out of conversations about a parent's failing health, or even the truth about the way they died. Some young people are excluded from funeral planning nor are they asked for ideas about memorializing their parent. Another need, then, is to be included in these conversations in a healthy and appropriate way. Similarly, the teen or young adult should be given a chance to help make decisions about memorial or funeral services or plans for ways to remember their parent.

Teenage and early adult years are a critical time for creating identity and meaning. Beliefs, spirituality, belonging, and understandings regarding fairness or justice in life are all a part of the mix. When a parent dies these issues and concerns are significantly affected and even tested. It's important for the young person, and the friends and adults who support them, to make sure these matters are not forgotten or set aside as one grieves and mourns. Often, the consistent help of a trusted adult—which may or may not be the surviving parent—is critical to the well-being of the grieving young person. This is a special need if the surviving parent, or other close adults, are overwhelmed by their own needs while grieving.

Although there are many issues that arise when a teen or young adult loses a parent, healthy grief and healthy adaption to the loss are certainly achievable with appropriate nurture, attention, and support. Being given the opportunity to be involved in planning the funeral or memorial service, encouragement to engage and talk about memories, fears, and hopes, and consistent support from adults and close friends are all helpful for life-nurturing grief process. It's also essential to encourage the young person to reflect on and talk about changes in roles and identity that may arise because of the loss.

9. . . . with the death of a grandparent?

The death of a grandparent could be the first significant loss of someone close that a young person experiences. Whether or not this is the case, such a loss can affect a teen or young adult in varying ways depending on family dynamics, the way their grandparent died as well as the way the family is able to cope with the death.

The loss of a grandparent will have a profound effect on the young person's own parent whose loved one dies. In fact, both parents could be dealing with significant loss depending on the relationship with the deceased, and they will likely have quite a bit to manage. For example, the surviving grandparent may be experiencing deep grief and need support from their adult children and in-laws. The son or daughter may need to deal with the estate of the young person's grandparent, or a move of the surviving grandparent may be necessitated. Among these and other issues that may arise, the teen or young adult's grief may be overlooked or given insufficient attention.

Other factors affecting the young person's bereavement will involve concerns that are typically present with the deaths of loved ones. The depth of the relationship the youth had with the deceased grandparent and the frequency of contact or connection can affect the intensity of grief. If the grandparent lived at a distance and the relationship was not well established, the feelings may not be as strong and the grief may last a short period. However, such a loss may still unsettle a young person. Sometimes the significance of the loss may not be realized until later—when the young person experiences milestones like graduation, marriage, children, buying a house, or other events that the family may share.

Other relational dynamics can influence the way a young person grieves the loss, such as whether the grandparent and grandchild enjoyed particular special events, as well as the relationship the deceased grandparent had with the young person's siblings. The relationship the deceased grandparent had with their child (the parent who lost their mother or father) can also influence the way the family grieves. The surviving spouse/grandparent's ability to cope, and even engage with the young person can affect the teen's grief and mourning. The death of one grandparent may also affect the relationship of the teen or young adult with the other set of grandparents. Closer relationships may occur, especially if other grandparents reach out to support the bereaved young person.

If the grandparent that died lived with the family, daily routines and family dynamics may especially be affected. Sometimes, a young person enjoys a deep bond with a grandparent they trust, especially if the youth has a strained relationship with their parents or if a parent suffers emotional or other challenges. In some cases, teenagers and young adults have been nurtured and supported by a grandparent, especially when a parent is absent or unavailable for various reasons. In all of these cases, the relationship lost when the supporting grandparent dies will be significant.

There are times when the grandparent passes away after a long illness or experiences a prolonged death. When this happens, there are many adjustments the family must make, especially if family members were intimately involved in day-to-day care, or if they visited often. Circumstances like these will also affect teens and young adults, since family dynamics will be affected. If the young person was allowed to be involved in the care, or visited frequently, coping with the loss could be less traumatic, depending on how well the family handled feelings and other matters surrounding their loved ones impending death. If the family dealt well with anticipatory grief (see Question 24), then coping after the death may be less stressful and the grief process more fruitful. The same may be true if a quality hospice care organization was involved. Hospice care, and the bereavement services offered after a loved one's death, can provide critical support for the family before and after the death of their loved one (see Questions 34 and 35).

Those who work with bereaved teens and young adults suggest other factors that can facilitate healthy grief after the death of a grandparent. The support given by parents, other adults in the family, as well as other grandparents still living is vital. "Giving permission" to grieve through healthy modeling is important. Talking about the death, showing emotion, or embracing other reactions and feelings as normal in the grief process is important for the family and may influence ways a youth may handle loss in the future. As with other significant deaths, including the teen or young person in funeral and memorial service arrangements and rituals of memory is crucial. The way the parents and family deal with the death may provide important life lessons regarding loss and how to cope.

10. . . . with the death of a friend?

There is a deeply held feeling that young people are not supposed to die. Many teenagers and young adults may feel immune from death or even that tragedy will not hit close to home. So, when a friend dies it is heartbreaking, life changing, and deeply painful. One's sense of fairness and personal identity are affected. A greater sense of vulnerability and a fear of death may arise. Some teens express feelings of emptiness, numbness, loneliness, and frustration when a friend dies, whether a close friend or not. Often a young person's beliefs and view of the world is shaken and challenged in ways not experienced before.

Friendships, especially close ones, can be more important to the teen or young adult than some family relationships. The parents may not know the deceased friend or understand the depth of relationship their son or daughter enjoyed with the young person that has died. In these cases, the parent may not have a full grasp of the loss or acknowledge the depth of feelings the young person may be experiencing. Appropriate support could be inadequate and the parents may wonder why the death is affecting their teenager in such profound ways.

Since friends are peers, a friend's death calls into question one's own mortality and brings the reality of death into sharp focus. Such a change in perspective and outlook can cause anxiety and confusion, but can also lead to growth, deeper awareness, empathy, and compassion. When a friend dies, mutual friends may band together after the death, seeking support and comfort while forging closer bonds. Sometimes though, such relationships may feel awkward and unsure and cause surviving friends to drift apart.

Other deaths, like the death of a grandparent or an adult relative, may fail to prepare a young person for the death of a friend or peer that has died. When a friend dies, there will be missed daily contact in school or hanging out on the weekends. Sharing other experiences is no longer possible and their absence could be overwhelming and cause intense discomfort. The surviving friends may begin to feel in acute ways that life will never be the same, and such a change will alter perspectives and affect other aspects of life.

As with other deaths, grief will most likely come in waves. There will be moments when you feel OK as well as times when the sadness, confusion, anger, or other feelings take control. It may be difficult to do homework or focus in school. Guilt and regret can also be a part of your feelings, especially if there was something you said or did that was critical or harmful, or that you wish had said or done, like expressing your gratitude for their friendship. Guilt can also arise in other ways, such as feeling there was something you could have done to prevent the death, or if you survived the accident that took the life of your friend. If you witnessed the death, then the trauma and grief responses can be more intense and prolonged (see Question 12).

In some instances, the circumstances surrounding the death of your friend are kept secret, or older adults may feel uncomfortable sharing facts or events. If the teen is treated as a child, or the older adults are afraid to address issues like suicide, or circumstances around accidents, or the uncertainties around illness and disease, then the young person may feel unanchored, as if there is no one they can trust. As in other deaths, being told in appropriate ways about the circumstances (not necessarily all the details) surrounding the death is critical. It is essential for the grieving young person that older adults tell the truth, even if the truth is "I don't know."

There are a number of ways to deal with one's grief (see Questions 21–37). When the death involves a friend, it is especially important to find outlets for grief and mourning. Attending the memorial service, though it may be difficult, can help the grieving process. If parents and family are supportive and understand, regardless of their awareness of the intensity of the relationship, they can offer vital support and care, simply by being present to listen or help. However, parents and other adults may not understand the depth of your feelings, and some friends may be uncomfortable dealing with death, so it is easy to feel isolated. It is essential then, when the time feels right, to talk about feelings with someone trusted. If parents are not able to provide the help needed, perhaps speaking with a teacher or counselor or other adult relative can be beneficial. Needing to be alone at times might be necessary, but prolonged isolation does not promote healthy grief. Talking about concerns like your fears, identity, changes in perspective, and issues around missing your friend with trusted individuals is critical.

11. . . . with the death of a child or the loss of a pregnancy?

The loss or death of a child is one of the most difficult losses one can endure. When a child or infant dies one's sense of fairness or understanding of the world is disrupted and our assumptions about how life is to unfold are shattered. These feelings and struggles may also arise when a pregnancy comes to an end spontaneously or is induced. When the parent is a teenager or young adult, the feelings of loss can be more problematic, depending on the circumstances surrounding their life and the pregnancy.

For many teenagers and young adults, losing a child may not be a part of their experience. However, statistics and estimates from several sources indicate a significant number of young women aged between fifteen and twenty-four will face the loss of a child or pregnancy. For example, in 2013 there were over 8,000 deaths of infants before the age of one for mothers twenty-four years old and younger. It's estimated that at least one in four pregnancies ends in a miscarriage, which translates to over 200,000 miscarriages for young women aged between fifteen and twenty-four in 2017.

Like the general population, teenagers and young adults may experience feelings of loss and grief due to miscarriages (before the twentieth week of pregnancy), stillbirths (after twenty weeks, but before or during delivery), legally induced abortions, complications before and after pregnancy (e.g., congenital malformations and chromosomal abnormalities, low birth weight and short gestation), sudden infant death syndrome (SIDS), and other issues. Some young adults may suffer the death of older children through accidents/unintended injuries, cancer, or other causes. Placing a child for adoption is a significant decision that can lead to grief and sadness as well. Each type of loss carries different implications for the grieving process. Though it would be difficult to cover each kind separately, a few will be described to highlight various concerns around bereavement and grief over the loss of a child or pregnancy. More information, hotlines and other resources can be found at places like the Office on Women's Health (www.womenshealth.gov) and The Compassionate Friends (www.compassionatefriends.org)

Someone who loses a child or infant would be expected to feel deep sadness, shock or anger, or even wonder "why me?" A teenager or young adult may feel a tremendous sense of guilt, believing something they did or did not do led to their child's death (as is often the case with SIDS), or be angry at God for taking their child. The loss of future hopes and plans can also lead to profound distress and pain. These and other grief responses described in earlier questions are possible, though each person will grieve differently (see Questions 2, 3, and 6).

Some losses are often more difficult to handle because of societal attitudes, cultural norms, or lack of understanding, leading to deeper confusion, isolation, and sadness for the grieving young person. Miscarriages and stillbirths are examples of such losses. When a young woman spontaneously aborts a fetus, those around her, even her closest family or friends, may fail to recognize the depth of her grief or that she may be grieving at all (see ambiguous or disenfranchised grief, Glossary).

Many times, the feelings of the father are ignored. Whether the pregnancy was planned or not, the expectant mother (and father) may have begun to feel a connection to the baby. The loss may be magnified if the young woman feels responsible for the miscarriage, while also grieving the loss of dreams for the child she hoped to birth. Feelings of self-blame and guilt can occur if the teenager or young adult believes that things like too much physical activity, or being careless with diet or medications, or working too much caused the miscarriage. Guilt can also arise if the young woman feels ambivalent or worried or scared about the pregnancy, believing such attitudes or emotional struggles had an adverse effect on the pregnancy. If the teenaged parents are unwed or minors, societal norms or family value systems could lead them to experience feelings of guilt and shame, which may intensify the experience of bereavement and grief.

Miscarriage is also difficult to talk about and acknowledge, and the silence about what has happened may lead to isolation and loneliness. Support from family, friends, and others are critical at these times, but if there is deep-seated guilt, or if some family and friends are judgmental, then opening up to conversations with loved ones and friends may be challenging or impossible. Others may not have known about the pregnancy, so if there is a miscarriage, it will be difficult to address the many feelings and concerns a young person may have. When some friends and family do know, the concern may turn more to the health of the mother leaving the significance of the loss unacknowledged. Well meaning, yet inappropriate comments are made at times—like "you can get pregnant again," or "you're lucky this happened" (if the pregnancy was unplanned or would cause major disruption in the young person's life). Such comments may be well intentioned, but lack empathy or the understanding a young person needs. Experiencing a miscarriage may cause the young woman to wonder if she can ever have a healthy pregnancy. A sense of relief may also occur, depending on the age and circumstances of the parents, if the pregnancy was unplanned, or if the parents are unable to care for a child. Relief, though, is a complex feeling especially around grief and loss. Some may feel guilty about experiencing relief, though it is an honest and often appropriate reaction (see Question 26).

Whatever feelings arise when a spontaneous abortion occurs, it's important for the teenager or young adult to acknowledge the emotions and responses. Turning to *trusted* family and friends is important and gives an outlet for talking, expressing feelings or simply being cared for by those who love you. It's also helpful to process feelings of loss with the other parent, if possible. Seeing the fetus is helpful for some, but not for others. Naming the fetus has also been a helpful way to grieve and cope, but not for all parents who have lost a pregnancy. Although there are few religious or secular rituals involving loss from miscarriage, it can be helpful to have a memorial service, or to do something else to memorialize the baby and acknowledge the loss (e.g., journaling, creating a memory box of items related to the expectant birth, planting a tree). If needed, there are hotlines, support groups, grief counselors, and other professionals that can help, especially if the young person's usual support are absorbed with their own issues around the pregnancy and loss. As with any grief process, looking out for one's own physical, emotional, and spiritual health is critical.

When a baby is stillborn, feelings that arise are similar to those experienced with miscarriages. However, since the baby is more fully formed there may be additional struggles. Some feelings, like the loss of hope and dreams for the newborn, or guilt, or difficulty being around healthy infants may be more intense. It may be more important for the parents and other family to hold the baby, name the child, and arrange for a memorial or funeral service.

Feelings of grief and loss also arise in the case of induced abortion. As with miscarriages, there are a significant number of young women who are affected each year. Data from the Centers for Disease Control and Prevention (CDC) indicate young women and teenagers aged between fifteen and twenty-four accounted for 41 percent of the estimated 638,169 induced abortions in the United States in 2015 (9.8% for those aged between fifteen and nineteen, and 31.1% for those aged between twenty and twenty-four). Although abortion is legal in the United States, there is often a stigma around the procedure and is denounced by a number of high profile political and religious groups. On the other hand, there are a significant number of individuals, organizations, and religious groups that support abortion rights and women who choose this direction. However, it is often difficult for women (and fathers) to know who to trust or where to go to process feelings, concerns, and decisions. Some problems arise because organizations designed to help process feelings and make informed choices like Planned Parenthood are inappropriately targeted and labeled by opponents. It is not surprising that young women may feel uncomfortable talking about or making public any emotions, concerns, discernment, or desire for support.

Because abortion is so politicized, feelings of isolation and greater sense of vulnerability may surface. These feelings may be intensified if the young woman is apprehensive or worried about telling the father, is unable to turn to parents or family, and reluctant to tell friends. For teenagers and young adults who are part of a religious community, feelings of shame may arise if the community offers judgment and condemnation, or if the young woman feels her own values will be tested by her decision. Fear, confusion, and anxiety can arise about the decision and the future. Many of these reactions are indeed tied to grief and loss. However, since induced abortion is viewed as a choice, the grief may be socially unacknowledged, or some might feel the person deciding to terminate the pregnancy has no right to grieve, or others may refuse to validate the loss (see ambiguous or disenfranchised grief, Glossary). Nevertheless, women who seek an induced abortion *have* a right and need to grieve and work through their loss.

One of the critical issues regarding bereavement around induced abortion is finding distance from the political debate. Like miscarriages, societal tensions and uneasiness about this kind of loss can limit important conversations around feelings, discernment, and grief responses. Curiously, one estimate indicates nearly one in two pregnancies are unintended or unwanted, so open dialogue around the multiple issues regarding reproductive health and choice should be highly valued, but sadly this is not the case. Consequently, it's very important to find emotional space to deal with the multiple feelings, thoughts, and concerns that arise around choosing an induced abortion. Finding a place for support may be difficult, but there may be family or friends willing to help. Hotlines, support groups, and health professionals are also available when needed.

A number of grief and bereavement experts note that for those contemplating an induced abortion, grieving actually begins with awareness of the pregnancy. It is then that feelings of loss arise, along with reactions like fear, blame, anger, guilt, and anxiety. So, it is suggested that conversation around bereavement and grief begin as soon as possible, so the young woman (and young father) can start to cope with responses and needed discernment regarding the pregnancy.

Often, there are worries around the emotional effects of the decision to terminate a pregnancy. Studies indicate the abortion does not pose a psychological threat for most women, though that does not mean the young woman (and young man) do not feel loss and grief. According to research the prevalent feeling after an abortion is relief. Relief in this instance is complex. It is often connected to feelings like hopefulness about the future, diminishment of worries about one's own health, and reassurance that the appropriate choice was made in light of all the circumstances. On the other hand, for women who contemplate or actually terminate a pregnancy, the feeling of relief can be accompanied by isolation and sadness, as well as confusion over mixed feelings. Isolation often occurs since few can understand what the young woman must face, and also due to societal attitudes and possible disapproval of those closest to her. Sadness is also probable, since this is a loss of a future as a mother with this child. Guilt may also accompany such a loss, especially if the decision to terminate the pregnancy in some way infringes upon the teenager's or young adult's religious, cultural, or ethical values (see Question 25). Some women may have to cope with shame, which arises from external attitudes and feelings of others—like family, society, church, or culture—and their attitudes about abortion. These and other emotions can reappear later in life as well, especially around another pregnancy, or in other circumstances involving children or family.

There are a variety of ways that a young adult or teenager can find ways to cope with a decision to terminate a pregnancy. In the beginning, it may be helpful to journal or create art, or do something that allows the young woman (and young man, if possible) to acknowledge and begin to deal with the feelings of loss and grief. If feelings of guilt arise, there are ways to seek forgiveness or an affirmative or healthy outcome. As noted before, it is also critical for young people to find a support system and those who can be trusted with the feelings that arise and the decisions that need to me made. Complicating the possibility for finding needed support, especially for adolescents, is that thirty-seven states require parental consent for minors seeking abortion. Even so, it is advised that teenagers seek help and counsel when one learns of the pregnancy so feelings and discernment can be handled in healthy and proactive ways.

Finally, another loss that is often ignored or given insufficient attention is the loss that accompanies a young person's decision to place a baby for adoption. As with other losses regarding the loss of a child or pregnancy, the feelings that arise can be confusing and complex, and the grieving process might begin when a young person becomes pregnant.

Many choose to place a baby for adoption for noble reasons. For example, a young mother may believe that adoptive parents can better care for the child, or that it is better for their baby to have two parents. Financial security, or the chance for sisters and brothers, or a stable family life may be hoped for the child. Whatever the reason may be, the decision to place a baby for adoption can also be fraught with ambivalence and feelings of loss and grief. These feelings are intensified and become more complicated if there is a poor support system, or immediate family members or a faith community create feelings of shame around the pregnancy. As a result, the young mother (and father) may also have to deal with exclusion or judgment along with their feelings of loss and grief. Additionally, an adolescent parent may be prevented from appropriate decision-making power regarding whether to see the child, or what future contact she or he may hope for regarding the child. Some young parents may be criticized for their decision, or ridiculed for their ambivalence or struggle with the decision. These and other issues are possible around placing a baby for adoption.

As with other situations that result in loss and grief, especially involving the loss of a child or pregnancy, it is important that the young person have a good support system. Often that support can come from understanding family, friends, and religious or other communities. It is also critical for the young mother and father to be thoroughly aware of the adoption process and the choices regarding future contact with the child. It's essential to deal with the loss of a future with the baby, perhaps by holding the child, making a way to create memories of the moment, journaling, taking pictures, asking the adoptive parents for pictures, and saying goodbye. Grief will involve being able to love and let go. Even though the decision to place a baby for adoption is good and appropriate, feelings of loss should be addressed and coped with in healthy, life-affirming ways. As with grief in general, healing and a new outlook on life is hoped for and possible.

12. . . . in the case of traumatic events or a traumatic death?

All losses are traumatic in some way, but there are deaths identified as *traumatic deaths* because of the circumstances involved. These circumstances have the potential to affect the grief response of a young person in ways different than that for more common types of loss. Grief, of course, is a unique experience for each person and not everyone will react the same. Some who experience a traumatic loss may grieve in usual ways and find ways to cope with little difficulty. However, bereavement specialists and practitioners have found that traumatic deaths present unique challenges to the bereaved and often overwhelm the capacity of the grieving young person (or adult) to cope.

Nicole Barlé, Camille Wortman, and Jessica Latack's scholarly article "Traumatic Bereavement: Basic Research and Clinical Implications," defines clearly and broadly these kinds of losses: "A death is considered traumatic if it occurs without warning; if it is untimely; it involves violence; if there is damage to the loved one's body; if it was caused by a perpetrator with intent to harm; if the survivor considers the death as preventable; or if the survivor regards the death, or manner of death, as unfair and unjust." Although comprehensive in scope others have added additional possibilities for this type of death and grief, such as the bereaved being involved in the circumstances surrounding the death (like an auto accident, natural disaster) or if they witnessed the death. Traumatic deaths, then, can span the range from homicides and suicides, to communal experiences like natural disasters, fires and mass shootings, to auto or other accidents, and to losses due to war and combat.

When a teenager is dealing with a traumatic death, they must cope with both trauma and grief. Each are distinct processes and are dealt with in somewhat different ways. However, the emotions and responses that arise from each may be hard to distinguish. For example, trauma responses often involve intense nightmares or worry about the safety of others. These responses can also be involved with grief, though less typical or severe than common reactions to loss like sadness, anger, and despair. However, for the young person who has experienced a traumatic death, all of these reactions may occur with greater frequency and intensity. Those grieving a traumatic death can develop PTSD which can involve nightmares and flashbacks, hypervigilance, worries about other threats, feeling intense and even explosive anger, difficulty trusting others, and concentration problems. Those with PTSD may also be more likely to shy away from reminders about friends and loved ones or similar circumstances that led to the death (like with complicated grief, Question 27).

There are other distinctive circumstances associated with traumatic deaths not typically experienced around other losses. For example, in the case of homicide or some other violent death, law enforcement will be involved. This can cause major disruptions in the bereaved person's life, especially if the incident occurred at home and the house is considered a crime scene. The grieving young person may be a witness, or a family member could be a suspect, which adds layers of issues and responses like anxiety, fear, intense anger, withdrawal, and confusion. If the person who committed the crime is at large, it is natural for the bereaved teenager or young adult (and family members) to feel a sense of fear and insecurity. All of these can interrupt the usual grieving process and add layers of trauma and associated responses.

When a crime is involved, a trial may also happen, which will typically raise anxiety and cause the bereaved to revisit feelings and emotions. Some may find difficulty grieving fully until the trial is over. If the young person is not connected to the trial or unable to attend, it would be important for the grieving teenager or young adult to be made aware of the trial's progress and outcome. Otherwise, anxiety and feelings of being isolated may arise and be more acute.

When there is a violent or traumatic death, media may be involved and community reactions, especially on social media, will be plentiful. Some media outlets may be supportive, while others are intrusive, insensitive, or rush to conclusions as to why the violence happened. Intense media attention, especially if it is unsupportive or unclear with the facts, will lead to isolation and distrust. In the case of natural disasters, widespread fires (like in California, Australia, and other locations in 2017–2020), or mass shootings the media attention will likely be excessive and overwhelming. In all of these circumstances, there are layers of grief and loss to deal with along with the trauma. In the Paradise, CA, fires of 2018, students, families, and the community had to deal with the death of friends, the loss of homes and livelihood, the loss of schools and school activities, losses due to friends and families moving, the loss of privacy, as well as other associated secondary losses.

When a loved one or friend dies in combat, a host of issues can arise. For example, there may have been an extended separation of the loved one from the family before the death, or a parent or friend is missing in action, or the circumstances around the death are muddled and confusing. In situations like these the young person may experience more intense feelings, ruminations, or trauma reactions.

Along with these special circumstances, there will be typical grief reactions and attempts to cope. All of these are natural, though it may feel more chaotic and overwhelming when paired with reactions to trauma. The bereaved teenager or young adult may feel constrained from speaking to friends for fear they will not understand, or because they are involved in the legal process, or simply because they do not want to share. Young people may feel numb and in shock, and experience strong feelings of sadness and anger. In the case of traumatic deaths, the teenager may imagine or play the incident over and over again in their head, or the young adult may feel the death is unreal. These are natural responses to loss, though they can become problematic if prolonged or entrenched. If the young person becomes obsessed with the circumstances and has trouble accepting and acknowledging the loss, they may experience longer periods of grief and mourning, or they may develop complicated grief (Question 27).

At a time when young people are developing their identity and worldview and finding ways to separate from the family in healthy ways, traumatic deaths can have a profound effect. A young person's sense of fairness, justice, predictability, and trust may be influenced. Spiritual values and beliefs may be tested and destabilized. Or, a young person may rely more heavily on spiritual comfort, or find inner resources they did not know they possessed.

Feelings of guilt or blame may arise, even if the bereaved had nothing to do with the death. Often, in the case of suicide, auto or other accidents, and other traumatic deaths, the young person may feel they could have done something to prevent the death or alter the circumstances that led to the death. Sometimes, guilt may arise because of the last thing a teenager said to the deceased, or a rift occurred in the relationship between the young adult and the person who died.

Finally, in the case of some traumatic deaths, there may be social unease around the circumstances and/or less social support. The bereaved may withdraw because the heaviness of the feelings and the turmoil they feel. The grieving teenager may feel shame because of the circumstances. Friends may have no idea how to help. Or, the bereaved young person may be avoiding conversation and memories due to PTSD or other trauma responses.

It might feel like traumatic losses will inevitably lead to hopelessness, complicated grief, or severe forms of PTSD or some anxiety disorder. However, there is hope and many who deal with traumatic death find ways to cope. Studies around well-known tragedies like Hiroshima in World War II, the severe acute respiratory syndrome (SARS) epidemic in 2003, and 9/11 have found that many people discovered ways to cope, survive, and grow emotionally, psychologically, and spiritually. However, there were those who needed more help to cope, especially if they witnessed the death of loved ones or some other traumatic event during these catastrophes.

Understanding that traumatic deaths can involve both grief and trauma reactions is critical to dealing with this special kind of bereavement. Learning about PTSD and when to seek necessary treatment can also be beneficial for dealing with the trauma and loss. Although PTSD is becoming more understood, there are times when those dealing with the disorder feel stigmatized and even ostracized. Being diagnosed with PTSD, or some other anxiety disorder does not mean the bereaved young person is weak or unable to handle the loss appropriately. PTSD can be an expected response to the intensity or duration of the trauma, especially if the bereaved witnessed the death or experienced the trauma as well.

Since trauma and grief are different processes, the way to treat and cope with them are different. In some cases, the different approaches and therapies may happen at the same time, while in others it may be best to deal with treatments around the trauma and then focus on issues around loss. Typical therapies for PTSD focus on certain types of psychotherapy, such as cognitive processing therapy (CPT) and prolonged exposure therapy (PE), to name a few, and medication. Research has indicated, though, that therapies are preferred and are more effective than medication in the case of PTSD. Unless the grief is complicated (see Question 27), or leads to other mental disorders, the remedies for grief do not require psychotherapy. Instead, telling stories about the deceased, journaling, being able to express anger or sadness in honest and healthy ways, and a number of other approaches are helpful to deal with grief (see below and Questions 30–37).

Since the stigma of a violent death or traumatic death may affect bereavement, it is important to keep channels of communication as open as possible. As with grief around other types of loss, sharing stories, positive memories and feelings with trusted friends, adults or a support group is helpful. The bereaved may have questions about the death and those who can provide information should do so honestly and appropriately. "I don't know" is an acceptable response when speaking to a grieving friend. Offering misinformation or withholding facts that can be appropriately shared can be harmful and disrupt the grieving process.

Outlets other than talking, like physical activity, journaling, making a video collage of the person who died, or other creative outlets are also beneficial. Similar to other losses, providing routine for the bereaved young person and making sure they have some choice regarding life concerns, the funeral, or other matters can help to give a sense of control and trust in the midst of chaotic feelings and events. In the case of violent deaths, it may be necessary to ensure that home and school is a place a teenager or young adult can feel safe. Finally, taking advantage of support groups in person and online, or professional help if needed, are invaluable. Processing the trauma is critical and may involve a number of evidence-based therapies that focus on cognitive, behavioral, and educational approaches as well as breathing/breath exercises and regulated exposure to memories and events.

A traumatic death of a loved one or friend will surely affect the kind and intensity of grief responses of the bereaved. Though grief is unique and every person reacts in different ways to loss, even with traumatic loss, it is essential to understand the possible reactions and how best to deal with them. What is most critical is to find support, share one's story, find healthy ways to grieve and get treatment as needed.

13. . . . in the case of suicide?

Many young people are touched by the trauma of suicide. Data from the CDC in 2017 indicate suicide was the second leading cause of death for those aged between ten and twenty-four, with nearly 7,000 young people dying by suicide. There were over 47,000 total suicide deaths in the same year. Although any death will cause sadness and pain, suicide is especially challenging to deal with. It is considered a type of traumatic death and is fraught with additional concerns (see Question 12). Research indicates that those grieving a suicide are at higher risk for PTSD, prolonged grief, and attempting suicide.

It's vitally important to take note of behaviors of a young person or friend grieving the loss of someone who died by suicide, especially if they have thoughts about taking their own life. In these instances, there are a number of signs to keep in mind. For example, if a bereaved friend is searching the internet regarding suicide, gathering means to take their life (e.g., drugs, firearms), are engaging in risky behaviors, withdrawing from friends and family, making plans, giving away things valuable to them, feeling hopeless and worthless, then it's important to ask the grieving friend or loved one if they are thinking of harming or killing themselves. Being able to listen in a nonjudgmental way is helpful for the bereaved person and gives an opportunity for a friend or loved one to offer understanding and compassion. It may be critical to seek help from adults, professionals, suicide hotlines, or to call 911 if there is a concern that harm is immanent.

Despite greater understanding about suicide and the needs of those at risk, suicide still carries an unwarranted stigma in society making the grief process more difficult. A suicide death is typically a shock to loved ones and friends and it frequently leads friends and family to wonder what they could have done to prevent it. Other responses that may occur when a loved one or friend dies by suicide are feelings of rejection, abandonment, or being unlovable. The question "Why" is a persistent and often haunting one, and almost always asked. Though it may seem like the death resulted from a single reason or precipitating event, the reasons are often numerous and complex. Whatever the reasons may be, those who die by suicide usually experience deep emotional pain, a profound sense of hopelessness, believe there are no options, and feel the only way to end the pain is to kill themselves. Some bereavement specialists disclose that those who have tried suicide, but lived, indicate their goal was to end the pain, not their life.

It's understandable, then, that grief responses around a suicide death may be more intense, prolonged, and difficult to cope with. It is not unusual for those grieving a suicide death to have a heightened sense of anger, especially when the questions around "why?" persist, or if there are strong feelings of abandonment or guilt. The bereaved teenager may be worried other friends or members of their family will also attempt suicide or that they may be at risk. Those in grief after a suicide may experience nightmares, have trouble concentrating, or deal with other issues around anxiety and stress (see Question 12).

A part of the normal grieving process usually involves making new meaning, which often entails sorting out the circumstances of a friend's or loved one's death. But, there will be a lot of questions around a suicide death, many unanswerable. In trying to make sense of the act, a young person may blame themselves in some way and think, "If only I had been with my friend . . ." or "I should have seen the signs. . . ." However, the suicide is not the fault of the bereaved. Even if the bereaved young person knows some of the reasons and circumstances, those clues do not tell the whole story or convey responsibility. Plus, it's impossible to read another's mind or sense what choices they will make. Sadly, the person who died by suicide was the one who took this action, and accepting this does not mean the bereaved loves them less, or lacks empathy for the depth of emotional pain experienced by the person who died.

In spite of these profound emotional obstacles new meaning and healing can be found, though it will be hard work. It is a process best done with the help of others who are supportive, since becoming isolated as one grieves is a danger. It is critically important, then, for bereaved teenagers and young adults who have lost a love one or friend to suicide to find someone who is open and trusted to talk with, whether an adult or support group. Since there is often a stigma around suicide deaths, the support needs to come from those who are able to listen compassionately, be nonjudgmental, and who are comfortable with various feelings and questions that may arise. It's essential that young people hear the truth about circumstances surrounding the death, although only the detail necessary and to the degree appropriate. Since a suicide often raises many questions, trying to protect the bereaved will be detrimental to their ability to cope. A young person may become preoccupied with filling in the blanks if there is a lack of information available to help them deal openly and honestly with the facts. Talking about suicide is actually more helpful than secrecy and silence, especially when facts and respected resources for education are included in the mix. "I don't know" is a much better response than misinformation.

Conversations around the risk factors for suicide, as well as sharing about how to cope with life's disappointments and difficulties, may also be needed and beneficial. Risk factors include things like previous attempts of suicide, a family history of suicide or abuse, experiencing major loss, history of mental disorders (e.g., depression, anxiety disorders), history of alcohol or drug abuse, suicide epidemics in the community, and access to lethal instruments (e.g., firearms in the home, access to potentially lethal drugs). Because there is still a stigma associated with suicide, dealing with education and understanding around risk factors and other issues is essential. Being sensitive with language used is one of the ways to diminish the stigma associated with suicide. For example, saying "a person committed suicide," implies moral choice or even a criminal act (like committing a crime), while saying "he died by suicide" moves away from judgmental language.

Hopefully, as a teenager or young adult grieves, the attention can be turned to the person who died and not the way they died. There will often be a need for young people to support one another, and be supported publicly if a fellow student or friend died by suicide. Possibilities include a moment of silence at school or some other ritual that honors the student that died while being sensitive about the circumstances of death. Funerals and memorial services may also be helpful. If acceptable to the family, mourning practices can involve education and awareness around suicide—but should not be expected. Whatever may happen, being given a chance to remember or tell stories about the friend or loved one can be a major help in the grieving process. As mentioned in other questions, routine can be helpful for young people as well as offering choices, especially regarding memorial services and how to remember the person who died. In some cases, it may be important to seek a qualified mental health professional, especially if there are major changes in behavior, the grief responses affect daily living, or the bereaved shows signs of wanting to end their life.

If you or someone you know is in crisis, please call the toll-free National Suicide Prevention Lifeline, 1-800-273-TALK (8255). It is a twenty-four hour, seven day a week service for anyone. For the deaf and hard of hearing, contact can be made through TTY, 1-800-799-4889. The Crisis Text Line is another resource available 24/7—text "HOME" to 741741. The Veterans Crisis Line is 1-800-273-8255 (Press 1 when prompted). All crisis lines and lifelines maintain confidentiality.

14. . . . with the death of a celebrity?

For some, a celebrity's death may lead to reactions similar to those of other losses. However, there are unique facets of a celebrity's death that might affect how a young person grieves. Grief over a celebrity death is a bit different because the bereaved does not actually *know* the celebrity on a personal basis. Yet, this does not necessarily diminish the loss one may feel. The intensity of grief has much to do with the connection or emotional attachment a person feels with the person (see Question 3). Young people and older adults may find connection to celebrities for a variety of reasons. The professional and personal life of musicians, sports players, actors, or other public figures are often public and easily accessible, so many people younger and older come to connect or identify with them in some way. Much of the connection is internal, or touches some part of us, or may influence one's identity. There are other examples of ways celebrities touch the lives of young people and older adults alike. The music and lyrics of a band's song may be experienced at critical occasion in life, or speak the feelings a young person may have inside, or shape the way a teenager or young adult sees the world or themselves. A character in a movie or show may be someone we admire and want to emulate, or they too may express thoughts about the world a young person may have. A public figure or politician may offer hope to young people and connect in ways other candidates fail to do. Or a blogger or podcast host may offer insight, new perspective, and connection for many followers.

Whatever the connection may be, when a celebrity dies it sometimes feels like a friend or family member has been lost, or as if a part of us dies. The feelings of loss can be heightened since the celebrity's death, or a preoccupation with details of their life saturates social media and news outlets. The loss is typically something shared with others in the community or the country or around the world. If social media or news outlets share in insensitive ways, the loss can feel more overwhelming. Care also needs to be taken around sharing on social media where positive *and* negative messages are communicated, or where the intensity of grief and the pain of loss can continue indefinitely (which is unhealthy). On the other hand, fans or followers can create a community of those who reach out and support one another in time of loss. If the celebrity is popular among teenagers and young adults, friends may identify pretty quickly with the grief they feel and the feeling of loss can be shared more easily.

The death of a celebrity may trigger memories and feelings associated with other losses, or may bring up other difficult feelings. For example, when the comedian and actor Robin Williams died by suicide, it was a significant loss for many in society. His death not only led to typical grief responses, but also highlighted concerns around suicide and the illness he suffered (Lewy body dementia). For others, his death may have sparked memories of loved ones who died by suicide or flashbacks of the experience. The death of musical artists may also bring up significant memories or other losses since their music may have shaped our views about self and the world, or be intimately connected to relationships, friends and loved ones, or major life events.

Be assured that grief over the death of a celebrity is normal and common. As with other losses, though, some may dismiss the bereaved young person's feelings, or try to hurry the grieving process along. However, teenagers and young adults have the right to grieve in healthy ways after a celebrity's death. The grief reactions will typically be like other losses. A bereaved teenager may feel shock, though the shock may feel more intense because celebrities often seem larger than life and invincible. The young person will likely feel sadness and anger, confusion and anxiety (especially if the death was a traumatic death, see Question 12) or find it difficult to concentrate or sleep.

It's important, then, for a bereaved young person to give themselves time to grieve and mourn. As with other deaths, it's important to get in touch with feelings and express them in healthy ways. Talking with or contacting others that are trusted or that can identify with the sorrow of the loss is critical. Since the death of a celebrity touches so many people, there may be ways online or in social media to express grief and find comfort. If it's possible to attend a public vigil or go to a memorial site, doing so is often beneficial and healing. As with a loved one who dies, sharing memories, or getting in touch with the memories of the person who died is helpful. Listening again to music or watching shows or movies connected to the celebrity who died can help the young person deal with their feelings. Keeping a routine can also ease feelings of turmoil or disorientation. Journaling and pulling together memorabilia are other helpful ways to cope with grief. However, if the grief goes on too long, or gets in the way of daily functioning, it is essential to seek additional help.

15. . . . with the death of a pet?

When a beloved pet dies, the grief is very real. The death of a pet is often the first significant loss that a young person suffers and some teenagers and young adults have reported that a pet's death is one of their deepest sorrows. There are accounts of bereaved pet owners, both young and old, who have grieved the loss of a pet more deeply than the death of a relative or acquaintance. However, the death of a pet is an experience that many do not understand or acknowledge as a significant loss. Even if others recognize the loss, they may not grasp the depth of grief that a teenager or young adult feels. "It was just a dog" or "you can get another cat" are often words offered without thinking, which underestimates the profound feelings and reactions that accompany the loss of a pet.

There are a number of reasons why the loss of a pet is so painful and difficult. A pet's unconditional love and acceptance is something young people and others feel acutely, and the loss of that love is a cause of anguish and sorrow. A pet is also with you every day, and you may spend more time with a beloved pet than others in your household. It's easier to "be yourself" around your hamster, cat, or other pet, and they often see a side of us that friends and family members may not see. Pets are also with us in challenging times and are a source of comfort and stability when facing hardships, relational stresses, or other losses. Our daily routines are defined by a close relationship with a pet, with customary and frequent moments for walks, feeding times, and play. A dog or cat may be a trusted friend, so the loss is more intense if a teenager's connection with parents or family members is strained, or if a young person is struggling with relationships with peers. Pets also have a subtle way of keeping us grounded and engaged in a healthier perspective and pace of life. Taking care of essential needs like eating, sleeping, play and companionship is a foundation for higher functioning and psychosocial development. All of these relational aspects of our bond with a pet are affected when they die, so profound grief over their loss is definitely understandable and normal.

What's also difficult about the loss is the pet is a special companion that the teenager or young adult took responsibility for and nurtured. So, the loss may feel like that of a caregiver, or to some degree someone acting in a parental role. These feelings will be especially intense at particular times, like when you return from school, or at a time when you went for a walk or had play time with your pet. Dealing with all the things associated with your pet, like a leash or food dish or aquarium, is also difficult, and just seeing these objects may be trying and painful.

The reactions that occur after the loss of a pet will be similar to those associated with other significant losses. A bereaved teenager may feel deep sadness, have trouble sleeping or eating, suffer from depression (mild or more severe), or feel like life has lost vibrancy and meaning. Those who grieve the death of a pet may even feel anger at the pet (if they didn't listen when called) or the circumstances or even God. Complicating grief are possible feelings of guilt, especially if the excruciating decision was made to euthanize the pet. A young person may feel they could have offered better care, thus avoiding the procedure, or be angry at parents for making the decision or failing to include their young person in the process. The teenager or young adult may feel responsible for the death in some other way, like leaving the door ajar allowing the pet easy access to the street, or failing to be attentive to signs of distress. The loss of a pet may also reawaken other losses, making it difficult to process and grieve in a healthy way.

Because euthanasia is fraught with complicated feelings and con-siderations more needs to be said regarding this aspect of a pet's death. The decision to euthanize is painfully difficult, even when the pet is in obvious distress and treatment will not improve their health or quality of life. What may help moderate some of the intense feelings that arise in bereavement is how those closest to the pet deal with this decision and action. If it does not cause too much distress, it is helpful to accom-pany the pet during the procedure, offering the same care, love and reas-surance given when the pet was healthier. Doing so may also help the pet owner avoid questions surrounding the procedure and how it affected their beloved pet. Of course, being with the dog, cat, or other pet being euthanized is only advisable for those young people who are of an age or maturity level to handle the emotions and memories that will emerge. It is especially helpful in this instance if family members offer support and comfort to each other as they surround the pet with love and care.

In whatever way the loss of a pet is experienced, the grief can be pro-found. What is helpful for bereaved teenagers and young adults are sug-gestions and resources similar to those available when someone suffers other losses. First and foremost, it is critical to be patient and practice self-care, doing things the pet may have taught—getting enough sleep, eating well, and dealing with basic needs. Acknowledging the depth of the loss and the accompanying feelings is also imperative for movement toward healing and acceptance. It's also important to seek out support from others, being careful to find allies rather than those who may judge the grief being experienced. Journaling about the life of your pet, writing a private eulogy, making a collage or memory book of pictures on the computer, or sharing stories with friends and supporters are other helpful ways to cope with the loss. Other rituals around burial, or spreading ashes, or other ceremonies and ways to remember are helpful activities for healthy grief. The young person may want to memorialize their pet in some way, which is an effective way to celebrate and remember their life and impact. There are a number of resources available online, in the community, and by phone for those who have experienced the loss of a pet. Young people and others grieving the loss of a pet can consult websites of organizations like the ASPCA, certain veterinary schools, humane societies, local animal hospitals, or the Association for Pet Loss and Bereavement (aplb. org). There are also telephone hotlines for those experiencing grief and who need someone to listen and offer support. These and other online and community resources can be found by simply doing a search under "pet bereavement" or similar phrase. Select websites and information are also listed in the resource section of this book.

Remember that grief over the loss of a pet takes time and takes its own course, just as bereavement with other significant losses. Healing and adaptation will come, as will a deeper appreciation for the love and relationship a teenager or young adult shared with a beloved pet.

❖❖❖

What Other Events Are Likely to Cause Grief and Mourning? What About . . .

16. . . . my parents' divorce?

There are other events and experiences that can lead to a profound sense of loss and grief besides losses through physical death. A parent's divorce can be one of the most distressing episodes in the life of children and young people. There is a relatively high number of divorces in the United States and its consequences is often given insufficient attention, especially for teenagers and young adult children. Because older children may be more mature, or even adults themselves, the feelings and effects of the divorce may be thought less traumatic. However, the feelings experienced by teenagers and young adults in a divorce are more likely to be similar to those of the divorcing parents, or like emotions suffered when there is a death of a family member (see Questions 7–9). Typically, there is more support from others and society in general when there is a death as opposed to a divorce, which may make it difficult to grieve in open, healthy ways. Attitudes about divorce or feelings of embarrassment can also affect the grieving process.

What makes grieving divorce so difficult is the sense that a "death" has occurred, though the parents are still physically present. Something important has broken and is coming to an end. There are many emotions often experienced like those when a death has occurred. For example, the children of divorced parents might struggle with feelings of guilt, believing they've done something to cause the marital difficulties, especially if they did something to cause major stress in the family. Or, teenagers and young adults might believe there was something they could have done to prevent the breakup. Anger and blame will typically well up, at times directed at the parent perceived to be at fault.

When a divorce occurs, household dynamics are disrupted and the young person will grieve the loss of routines and consistency, even if dysfunction was a part of their everyday family life. The teenager or young adult might feel relief that the arguing and conflict has diminished. However, such feelings may also lead to pangs of guilt for responding this way. Some young people may suffer major shock, especially if there were few visible signs of discord. The children of divorced parents will also need to adjust to many changes and concerns, including living arrangements, financial worries, negotiating family events, and potentially diminished opportunities for their future. Some young people may be expected or feel compelled to become a "head of household" figure, or they may be caught in between the parents' ongoing conflict. These reactions and issues can cause confusion and emotional turmoil for the young person and may prolong the grief response. One of the significant losses is a sense of stability which is important for teenagers and young adults. A stable family environment can provide a foundation that allows a young person to feel safe and explore the world, and work to develop identity. But, if a relationship a teenager or young adult depends on comes to an end, it can make healthy development more difficult. All of these feelings can be intensified if the terms of the divorce decree stipulate limited contact with one of the parents, or a parent needs to move for some reason (like a job), or the divorce leaves a parent emotionally depleted.

There are other issues that may complicate the grief response. In some cases, parents have stayed together for the sake of the children only to divorce when the children are older and, in the parents' minds, able to handle the breakup. But, separation and divorce are just as devastating for teenagers and young adults, especially as they are preparing to seek new adventures in life and establish their own identity. There may be a heightened sense that they need to take care of one of the parents, especially if the parent unexpectedly struggles with the circumstances surrounding the divorce. Feelings may also arise that the parents have been living a lie and lead to a lost sense of trust. If the parents modeled a marriage that was unloving and sterile, the consequence and attendant feelings could also affect healthy grieving and development.

A teenager's experience of grief around their parents' divorce can be more difficult if infidelity or an affair is involved. As in any divorce, the world the teenager knew and depended on is distressed, but an affair can heighten the trauma. If the young person was aware of the infidelity, deeper issues could arise regarding grief and coping. In either case, feelings of anger, distrust, and shame can develop, especially if the affair is made public. Anger could be directed at the offending parent, disrupting the relationship between parent and young person. If the teenager is the same gender as the parent having the affair, identity issues could possibly evolve. There may be greater anxiety about the future, especially if the extramarital relationship continues. Experiencing a divorce due to infidelity may also affect how a teenager or young adult views relationships, interrupting the development of healthy relational feelings, boundaries, and commitment.

Issues may surface when parents begin dating again after the divorce, or as casual dating with someone moves toward a more serious relationship. Unresolved feelings could arise, such as a longing for parents to get back together (even if unacknowledged), or feelings of anger and distrust or concern about how long the new relationship may last. As with other types of bereavement, grief around divorce can become more problematic and complicated, leading to feelings of depression, substance abuse, and risky or harmful behaviors (e.g., skipping classes, self-harm, eating disorders).

Finally, when a teenager or young adult suffers a significant loss, parents who provide a stable environment are often allies and support as the young person copes with their feelings. However, in the case of divorce, one or both parents may be emotionally unavailable as the teenager or young adult child attempts to process feelings and responses. Sometimes a parent's grief, anger, or confusion is too overwhelming to be a comfort and help. Or a parent may have already moved on emotionally, especially if they've dealt with issues around their marital relationship for a long period of time.

Although the divorce of one's parents can certainly be traumatic and source of ongoing grief, there are many teenagers and young adults who have found a way to cope, adjust, and thrive. There are several things that can influence a healthy grieving process and allow for hope and change. As with other bereavement, the parents can be critical to the support of the young person and their ability to cope with multiple losses that occur around a divorce. Even though a parent may be suffering, it is important they give space and guidance for their teenager or young adult child as they grieve. It is a difficult parenting responsibility, but offering love, support, understanding, listening, and a chance to share or vent can go a long way in helping the teenager and young adult to find healing amidst their anger, hurt, and fear. How the parents manage the separation and divorce and decisions that must be made are also important as the young person grieves. Giving appropriate decision-making power to their teenager and young adult can be helpful with so many changes on the horizon. For example, simply allowing the young person(s) to be involved in looking for a new place to live can help them deal with the loss of the home they knew. It's essential that parents reflect on and speak the truth clearly and gently, especially when asked questions that are appropriate to answer. It's also helpful for parents to be reassuring, make clear boundaries with an ex-spouse, avoid using children as go-betweens, resist blaming or speaking badly about an ex-spouse, and keep lines of communication open. Parents should encourage respect of their ex-spouse, but also be open to simply listening when the teenager is frustrated or angry with the other parent. It's also important to give attention to important dates, birthdays, and holidays in ways that honor the feelings and hopes of the young person, as well as help to create new family experiences around holidays and special occasions when appropriate.

Other trusted adults and family members can be important allies as the teenager grieves. They need to be persons who listen well, are engaged in the process, and can offer nonjudgmental responses as the young person examines their feelings and responses, or simply needs to vent. Friends who may have experienced the divorce of their parents, support groups, or counselors and other mental health professionals can be helpful as the teenager deals with the mix of feelings and thoughts that accompany such a loss. As with other losses, the way a young person grieves when their parents' divorce will be unique to the bereaved. Of course, there should never be an assumption that the divorce of parents will inevitably lead to emotional problems later for young people. However, it is critical that the teenager or young adult find the help they need as they cope with the divorce and losses it brings.

17. . . . sexual assault?

The Office of Women's Health (U.S. Department of Health and Human Services) defines sexual assault as "any type of forced or coerced sexual contact or behavior that happens without consent. Sexual assault includes rape and attempted rape, child molestation, and sexual harass-ment or threats." When speaking or writing about sexual assault, grief is not a term that usually comes to mind. However, sexual assault and abuse involves many losses and some of the feelings and responses that emerge after an assault are indeed grief reactions.

The grief associated with sexual assault is considered *ambiguous grief* or *disenfranchised grief* by some bereavement experts (see Glossary), because it's often difficult to perceive, does not involve the physical death of a loved one or friend, and is too often unacknowledged as loss by soci-ety. However, dealing with the grief that accompanies sexual assault and abuse is critically important for teenagers and young adults, especially young women. Statistics indicate that one in five women have been the victim of rape, and 40–50 percent of rape cases involve female teenagers fourteen to nineteen years old. Over half of women have suffered sexual assault of various kinds. Though the majority of assaults and abuse are committed against women, boys and men are also victims, with esti-mates of 15–20 percent of males being assaulted or abused before they reach the age of eighteen. Statistics regarding sexual harassment indi-cate that around 80 percent of the victims are women and 20 percent men. Although the sexual assault epidemic is gaining more attention in society, many persons and communities are ill-equipped to deal with the issues that accompany assault. In addition, too many communities, persons, and government officials are silent or resist changes in attitudes and laws that would better protect and help assault survivors, especially on college campuses. Such attitudes and resistance make it more diffi-cult for sexual assault victims in schools and colleges to safely tell their story, find justice, and move to healing and hope. Because of the varied reactions to assault, and that many societal responses are inadequate and poorly informed, the ability for survivors to grieve in healthy ways is difficult.

One of the difficulties when a young person has suffered sexual assault or harassment is having to deal with trauma and grief. Although there may be some overlap in feelings and ways to cope, trauma and grief involve different processes and remedies (see Question 12). What is critical in both instances is to make sure the victim is able to deal with reactions and emotions in a safe environment. It's also important that the bereaved young person be involved, as much as they are able, in making choices and decisions about direction and ways of dealing with the loss, pain, and distress. Other concerns like trust and cultural sensitivity are also part of dealing effectively with trauma and grief. Those supporting the victim of an assault or harassment should become aware of or practice trauma-informed care (see Glossary). Helpful information can be found at the CDC website (www.cdc.gov/cpr/infographics/6_principles_trauma_info), the National Child Traumatic Stress Network (nctsn.org), and the Sanctuary Model developed by Dr. Sandra Bloom (sanctuaryweb.com).

A person who has suffered some form of sexual assault will go through emotions and reactions that are typical grief responses. Often, the victim will experience denial that the assault really happened, or that the person who committed the assault could actually do so. However, over 70 percent of rapes are committed by someone the victim knows. Oftentimes the survivor believes the assault was their fault. Sexual assault IS NOT THE FAULT of the victim! Some friends, family, and others may fuel the denial because of the circumstances surrounding the assault (e.g., a party, alcohol or drugs involved, romantic overtures), or because the survivor knew the perpetrator, or because the perpetrator is known and family or friends refuse to believe they would commit assault or abuse. Unfortunately, such feelings simply isolate the survivor and discourage sharing their pain or reporting the assault.

Anger is certainly felt after an assault, though not immediately since many assault survivors are in shock. It's well known that those who report assault are often matter-of-fact or stoic in their reporting, which is related to the shock and numbness felt after an attack (which is sometimes a way to protect the survivor from overwhelmingly intense emotions). The anger can be directed toward many people other than the perpetrator. For example, anger can arise if a teenager or young adult is left alone by friends at a party or in other circumstances when they are most vulnerable, or friends abandon the survivor after the assault when understanding and care are deeply needed. The survivor can be mad at themselves, believing they are responsible for the attack or were careless with decisions. The young person can be irritated with the family for their lack of understanding, feelings of disappointment, or for blaming the survivor. Some survivors blame God, a higher power, or authority figures for allowing the assault to happen or for not having safeguards in place.

The person who has been assaulted may have difficulty eating and sleeping, or experience other health issues. They may find themselves crying uncontrollably when a conversation or activity triggers their deep and often silent grief. Nightmares, flashbacks, concern for safety are all responses associated with grief and trauma.

The teenager or young adult who has suffered an assault may feel guilt and shame (see Question 25) because of perceived responsibility, or because of societal attitudes and ignorance. Guilt may arise if the survivor feels they have caused pain for loved ones. Issues can also surface in later romantic relationships because of the trauma experienced, and the young adult or teenaged survivor may feel guilty when these issues get in the way of a healthy relationship. It is not surprising, then, that those who have suffered assault feel the weight of their own feelings as well as other's inappropriate judgments and misunderstanding.

Unfortunately, there is an unwillingness by too many in society to fully and adequately address the prevalence and consequences of sexual assault. Assault is often treated as a taboo subject and shrouded in secrecy. Other losses, such as the death of a loved one or friend, are usually validated and the bereaved supported. Such validation promotes and supports healthy grief. The bereaved may cope through sharing stories and memories. However, sexual assault and abuse are uncomfortable to talk about and difficult, even for the survivor, to acknowledge. Often the assault and accompanying losses are left unvalidated, while memories are fragmented or haunting. Inadequate societal and personal reactions lead the bereaved survivor to experience a greater sense of loneliness, confusion, and abandonment. Secrecy, or treating assault as a taboo, also intensifies a sense of mistrust, and deeper feelings of anger, frustration, and depression.

There are many loses associated with sexual assault and abuse. The survivor may feel a loss of: innocence; a sense that the world is safe; future possibilities; healthy sexual identity or a sense of healthy romantic relationships; one's self-identity or place in the world; trust in family or friends or the ability to relate to someone as a trusted friend; trust in self, especially if teenaged survivor believed it was their fault, or a belief they are not able to care of themselves; faith; trust in men. There is also a loss of control of one's own story or the narrative around their sexuality. In high schools or college campuses, assault victims are sometimes victimized again by rumors and false narratives about their sexuality, who they are, or what may have happened.

For the teenager or young adult who has suffered sexual assault, life can be viewed in a compartmentalized way, separated into "before the sexual assault" and "after the sexual assault," with attendant problems and issues around healthy, age-appropriate development (social, psychological, emotional, relational, spiritual).

For families and friends that are supportive, they too suffer grief emotions and reactions, and often are unsure what to do or how to help. There is also a loss for the community at large when the perpetrator is well-known, a loved one, or admired. Those grieving may feel anger and frustration, and feelings of mistrust and betrayal. When the appalling and criminal behavior by the perpetrator does not make sense, or seems out of character, the incongruence is unsettling, and the grief process difficult to handle. Young people in high schools or on college campuses may deal with this kind of loss when a fellow student, teacher, or popular celebrity has assaulted or harassed someone.

PTSD is a strong possibility for those who have experienced sexual assault and though PTSD symptoms are different from usual grief responses, some overlap with normal grief reactions and complicated grief may occur (see Questions 5, 12, and 27). Thoughts of suicide may also haunt the assault survivor.

Although the possible reactions and responses mentioned above are daunting, there are ways to find help from those who are caring, compassionate, and willing to listen. There are trusted family and friends who will be supportive and numerous bereavement and mental health professionals that can assist the grieving process, help deal with the trauma, and aid the survivor to find ways to heal and thrive again. Support groups are available in person or online. Those who have suffered assault and coped with the difficult feelings and reactions are also willing to reach out, share stories, and be companions with those who need to heal. A young person's faith can be a comfort. Journaling may allow the survivor to get her or his story out into the world in a private way.

What is critical for the teenaged or young adult survivor is to focus on self-care, finding appropriate support, and dealing with the many emotions and reactions in ways that promote healing and resilience. When the time is right, other ways to cope with the feelings and experiences around assault include becoming involved in helping others through survivor networks or volunteering at a domestic violence shelter. Blogging at various websites for survivors or sites that provide information around sexual assault has also been helpful for those who have experienced an attack. Finding one's voice and speaking one's truth in places and with those who will offer nurture and support can also help the survivor find peace and acceptance. Doing so may also help others who have suffered assault or harassment. It's also important for the survivor to find ways to take control of their bodies and strive for a healthy self-image. As some survivors and counselors advise, it is important to recognize that the assault does not define the survivor—it happened to them and is not who they are.

If you or someone you know has suffered sexual abuse or assault, please contact the sexual assault hotline, 1-800-656-HOPE (4673), or if in danger or injured call 9-1-1. The National Domestic Violence hotline is 1-800-799-SAFE (7233). Other contact information and resources are listed in the Directory of Resources at the end of this book.

18. . . . bullying?

The CDC provided a uniform definition of bullying in 2014 that focuses on different criteria, modes and types. According to the CDC, bullying is a form of youth violence that results from any act that is unwanted aggression from another youth, involves a power imbalance either observed or perceived, and that is repetitious or is very likely to be repeated (the definition excludes violent acts by siblings and current dating partners which are categorized under domestic or intimate partner violence). The bullying can be direct or committed in the presence of the victim, or indirect such as through social media or spreading rumors. The types of bullying fall into three broad categories: physical (hitting, pushing), verbal (name calling, teasing, and other verbal abuse), and relational (spreading rumors, social exclusion). Bullying can also involve damage of property and can be associated with criminal acts like harassment and assault.

The 2017 statistics from the National Center for Education Statistics and Bureau of Justice and the CDC indicate that approximately 20 percent of teenagers experienced bullying. Around 15 percent of teenagers reported being the victim of cyberbullying. 70 percent of students and 70 percent of school staff have seen bullying occur on campus. Other sources indicate 30 percent of teenagers have been involved with bullying another person. Statistics show the menacing presence of bullying in the lives of young people. Yet statistics do not tell of the real harm to those who have been bullied and the bystanders who watch.

There are a number of behaviors and emotions that emerged in early human development that helped humanity to survive and thrive. Some of these emotions and behaviors are closely related to loss and grief. For example, both anger and sadness (see Questions 23 and 28) are typical reactions to bereavement and likely evolved early in human history as responses to harm and threats (anger) or to pain, sorrow and loss (sadness). These emotions, as well as grief, are part of being human.

Likewise, integral to our humanity is the notion that we are social beings, wired to be in relationship with others. Bullying, at its core, touches the victim at the heart of their humanity since bullying focuses on intentional harm and exclusion which results in a loss of connection to peers and social interaction. The victim of bullying, then, will not only need to deal with the trauma of being bullied, but will also experience grief. Besides loss of relationship with the group, victims of bullying suffer other losses like the loss of respect, safety, trust, self-respect, and educational opportunities. Because of these multiple losses, the victim has a greater potential to struggle with grief, and the grieving period could be more prolonged, especially if the bullying continues.

The victim will experience normal bereavement reactions like anger and sadness, though they could be more intense due to the trauma endured. The victim may lash out at others or become hostile, or they may turn the anger inward and become self-destructive or harm themselves. In an attempt to avoid more mistreatment and harm, the victim may try to make deals with the bully, or with the parents to avoid going to school. Varying degrees of depression, withdrawal, sleeplessness, trouble eating, difficulty with schoolwork, risky behaviors, and denial may also occur. Denial is especially thorny since the victim can have difficulty accepting they were in fact a victim. They may laugh it off, make excuses for the perpetrator, or become uncertain. Since the bully has the power, and is usually self-confident, the disparity between the emotional and behavioral responses to the intimidating act may isolate the victim even more. Because bullying often makes the victim feel worthless and alone, deeper forms of depression are more of a possibility. The reactions and behaviors of the bereaved victim may escalate and lead to more serious forms of grief (see Questions 27 and 29), depression, or attempts to end their pain through suicide.

Witnessing trauma is scary and unnatural and can be difficult to process and deal with as well, so bystanders are also susceptible to feelings typical of the bereaved. Fear, higher levels of stress, emotional overload and fatigue, and feelings of guilt and shame are typical responses of the witness to bullying. As a result, the bystander may grieve the loss of self-respect, friendships, a sense that the world is safe and innocence. Even the few bystanders who act to help the victim can experience feelings associated with loss and grief. Although the grief responses may not be as intense or prolonged as that of the victim, dealing with these feelings in proactive ways is essential for healing, growth and developing empathy and courage in the face of other bullying episodes.

It is essential for the victim of bullying to find and be given help to deal with the trauma and grief. Research identifies long-term effects for the health and well-being of the victim if interventions are inadequate or absent. These include PTSD, major depression and other mental health problems, eating disorders, self-harm, and suicide. Since the bystander can also experience trauma and loss, they too can suffer long-term consequences such as PTSD and other issues that affect their physical, emotional, and spiritual well-being. The long-term effects have been found to be related to the bystanders' exposure to the abuse, resilience (see Question 36), and the potential they may be harmed. For the victim, long-term effects can occur regardless of duration since they have suffered directly from trauma.

There are a variety of ways to help the victim of bullying that touch on their grief and loss. One of the basic ways to help is to become aware of the facts about bullying. The websites for the CDC (cdc.gov) and stop-bullying.gov are excellent resources. Although any youth can be bullied, it is also important to be aware of targeted groups (e.g., youth that are new to a community; youth that are socially isolated due to appearance, disability, mental health issues, and other reasons; lesbian, gay, bisexual, transgender, queer or questioning [LGBTQ] youth).

As with other forms of trauma, it is essential to help the victim seek medical attention if needed, as well as attend to emotional needs. Friends and family can help the victim face grief and loss by listening in non-judgmental ways and allowing the young person bullied to express their feelings and needs. Appropriate questions may need to be gently asked so to help the victim understand and be clear about the ways the perpetrator crossed boundaries and did harm. Helping the bereaved victim focus on positive activities and experiences is also important, not as a way to ignore the trauma and grief, but to give the bereaved victim a chance for a needed breath and break from the grief (see Questions 3 and 28). Such activities may also aide the grieving process and help the victim regain a sense of hope and control.

It's also critical for the young person who has been bullied to find or develop a supportive network of friends, as well as rely on supportive adults. Research shows that the lack of friends or support groups is a risk factor for being victimized. Support groups are also critical in the grief process, offering a safe place to express feelings, talk about issues and concerns, and temper the desire to withdraw or feel isolated. Since bullying involves trauma and grief, it may be helpful to seek the help of a therapist adept at dealing with the effects of trauma and bereavement, especially if the victim develops PTSD, depression, or other emotional or mental disorders. At the very least, parents, supportive adults, and friends can help the victim deal with self-deprecating thoughts and encourage positive inner messages. It is also very important for friends to be in touch with adults, hotlines, or emergency personnel if the victim begins to exhibit signs of self-harm or suicide (see Question 13).

The bystander may also need to deal with feelings of grief and loss. Many of their reactions and internal responses may be connected to feelings of fear or guilt due to inaction during the bullying incident. Those who witness the bullying may need to share their frustrations, stress, anger, and fear with those who will listen without judgment. Finding ways to help victims, especially if the bullying continues, can be beneficial to the witness as well, and may help deal with feelings of helplessness and guilt. Simple acts like moving closer to the victim, body language, disapproving facial expressions, or telling a teacher or other adults can be effective in disrupting aggressive acts. Encouraging others to band together to protect the victim can also help. Statistics indicate that bullying stops within ten seconds in over half the occurrences when bystanders intervene. Speaking to the teenager that has been bullied, whether they are a friend or not, to offer support, empathy, and compassion can benefit the victim and bystander as well.

Parents are in a unique position to support and encourage their teenaged son or daughter who is being bullied. It is critical for the parent to listen and be willing to discuss issues around bullying, to ask needed questions and to recognize signs of being bullied. Hopefully, parents will be proactive in developing or encouraging compassionate and supportive social environments for their son or daughter, such as encouraging friendships, working with school teachers, staff and administrators, limiting access to violent media or firearms, as well as connecting their teenager to appropriate emotional, spiritual, and psychological support. It is also essential for parents to practice good self-care and seek the help they need, for they too will experience grief and loss. What is not helpful, and most likely harmful, is for parents to ignore, dismiss, or blame the young person victimized for the attack.

Schools can also work to create environments to reduce incidents of bullying and to provide safe places for victims through management of classes, handling incidents of bullying with compassion and dignity, dealing with threats of violence or counter-violence, encouraging empathy, and seeking the wisdom of evidence-based programs focused on bullying. It's also important for teachers, counselors, and staff to be trained around issues of youth violence, and for counselors to provide a safe place for victims to vent and share their feelings.

Since bullying is a traumatic experience, it is important for the victim to deal with the trauma as well, and for them and others to be aware of the signs of deeper issues and problems that lead to PTSD, serious mental disorders, or complicated grief (see Questions 5, 12, and 27). As with others who face grief and trauma, it is possible for a victim of bullying to find hope, health, and new meaning, while developing stronger coping techniques and ways to interact with the world. However, it is a journey that's best taken with the support of others who can encourage, listen, offer help in tangible ways, provide a safe place of acceptance, and offer assurance of worth and dignity.

19. . . . a breakup with a girlfriend, boyfriend, or partner?

Grief is a natural response to loss, and there are circumstances and events other than death can cause powerful grief responses. One of the most common losses a teenager or young adult may experience is the loss or end of a romantic relationship. The emotions and reactions that arise after a breakup can be intense and significant. The loss can feel agonizing in the first days and weeks or longer. The pain and isolation can feel weightier since this type of loss is often experienced as *disenfranchised* or *ambiguous*, which means the loss is unacknowledged, thought to be insignificant, or is socially stigmatized by friends of one or the other partner. Interestingly, the intensity of grief typically has less to do with the length of time the relationship lasted than the closeness developed in the relationship. Unfortunately, many older adults fail to understand the depth of feeling teenagers and young adults experience around relationships, or simply dismiss the loss. Parents and older adults might say that "you're young, you'll find another relationship," or "you're too young to really know what love is." Or, the bereaved young person may hear from some friends and adults alike "you're better off without them," or "time heals all wounds." Such comments are unhelpful and ignore the pain of loss. Since parents and families often model ways of coping when there is a loss, giving less attention to the grief experiences after the end of a relationship can adversely impact the young person's ability to deal with the loss.

There may be quite a number of grief responses after a relationship ends. Many teenagers and young adults will experience reactions typical for grief like anger (sometimes intense), sadness, loneliness, frustration, sleep difficulties, loss of control, or mild depression. A young person may walk around in a fog, as if the world is a little off, and feel like everyone is moving on and ignoring their pain. If the bereaved shares classes at school with the former partner, or they see each other often in hallways or on campus, it is a constant reminder of the loss. Academic performance may suffer for a time and the grieving young person may feel the need to withdraw. Any person who suffers a broken relationship (young people and older adults alike) may wonder if they will find love or a committed relationship again. There is also a higher risk for self-medication or other risky behavior.

The depth of grief depends in some part on the level of attachment (see Question 3) and the emotional energy invested in the relationship. The breakup also comes at a time in the young person's life when relationships of any kind are of prime importance. A broken relationship can also affect a young person's sense of personal identity, or the identity developed as a couple. Hopes and dreams regarding the future can be altered.

Other reactions associated with the end of a relationship may also occur. The bereaved may be confused about the reasons for the breakup, feel unlovable, or become isolated. The young person in the relationship who did not anticipate the breakup may feel like a failure or inadequate. They may feel guilt for having done something to harm the relationship, or failing to do something to preserve it. The bereaved may also feel guilty for having such intense reactions when those around them seem unfazed by the importance and depth of loss. Some may experience such a loss as a kind of death since the end of a significant relationship often feels as though something inside has perished.

Since the relationship that ends is not likely a marriage, or does not usually involve the couple living together, it may fail to register as something significant for others. Even so, the breakup may be public or talked about on social media. Others may be quick to blame or criticize one of the young people in the relationship, which can add to the pain, sadness, and isolation. Secondary losses may also occur, like severed ties with friends or the family of the former partner, or keeping distance from events or places enjoyed together as a couple.

Dealing with the loss of a significant relationship may be affected by how the young person has coped with other losses, or how they may have developed resilience in other ways (see Question 36). However, there are a number of ways a teenager or young adult can find help for grieving in healthy ways. As in other losses, finding friends, family, or trusted adults to talk with that understand the realness of the pain and the grief are important, since it is critical for the bereaved to express their grief and sadness and to share other thoughts and feelings that arise. Although there are times and good reasons for the bereaved to be alone, it's important to strike a balance with such a need by staying connected with others. Becoming isolated in unhealthy ways can be detrimental to the grieving process and in finding ways to cope and heal. Hopefully, the grieving teenager and young adult can begin to find meaning in life beyond the relationship and come to embrace a positive sense of self and their dignity. The grief process can also be a time to develop a deeper awareness of what one hopes for in future romantic relationships. Finding other outlets like journaling, exercise, spiritual resources, having fun with friends, enjoying nature or another interest (hobbies, movies, reading), or reaching out to help others can also be tremendously helpful. Above all, it is important to practice self-care physically, emotionally, and psychologically and find ways to cope with the loss. Of course, if the sadness, depression, or other responses become acute and interrupt daily functioning for too long, the young person may need to seek help with a bereavement or mental health professional. No matter how one responds to a breakup, it's essential to be patient, take a step at a time, and do what is needed to deal with the loss.

20. . . . the loss of hopes and dreams?

One type of loss that may be ignored or thought less significant is the loss of hopes and dreams. However, a young person can be deeply affected when hopes and dreams fade and, coupled with other losses, can make the grieving process muddled and more difficult. There are numerous ways a teenager or young adult can experience bereavement around future possibilities or aspirations. Sometimes the event or circumstance is the primary loss for the young person, like being turned down for acceptance into one's first choice for college (or suffering several rejection letters). Such losses can also be felt if the young person finds themselves ill-suited for an expected major in college or career direction. Perhaps a teenager loses a good paying job that fit well around school responsibilities, or a young adult does not get the dream job that seemed attainable. Grief can emerge when an anticipated scholarship, either sports related or academic, does not come through, or when a diagnosed illness might affect a young person's hopes and future possibilities.

The bereaved teenager or young adult dealing with such losses will likely experience typical grief emotions and reactions. Shock, sadness, anger, preoccupation with the loss, anxiety, problems with eating and sleeping, fear, struggles with school, and withdrawing may be felt or endured to varying degree or intensity. In some cases, the young person may have mild feelings of sadness or upset, but be able to move on quickly to what needs to be done next. Others may take longer, depending on the emotional investment in the particular school or job, and especially if there is an illness or other factor involved that will affect the young person's future or grief process.

Many times, the loss of hopes and dreams is secondary to another significant loss. For example, the loss of a parent (see Question 8) can be a devastating loss to the family, particularly the teenager or young adult. Often, a change in the financial circumstances accompany such a loss, which could affect hopes and dreams for the future. Going to college might need to be put on hold, or a teenager may need to drop out of college if the situation warrants. In situations like these others may question the young person's concerns in the midst of the loss of a loved one.

Feelings of guilt might result and cause the bereaved to set aside other losses, like dreams for the future, which may not be the best or healthiest way to cope. Sorting out the jumble of feelings in healthful ways with those who will listen and be nonjudgmental is most helpful, especially in light of what the teenager or young adult needs.

A parent losing a job, or a fire, or natural disaster, can also affect financial circumstances and delay hopes and dreams about school or a career. Such events will cause enormous stress for parents who are dealing with their own grief and the practical consequences of the loss. Hopefully, the parents will find the help they need so healthy grieving and self-care can be modeled. It's critical for adults to provide space for young people to express grief reactions and emotions and talk about fears and needs. It's also important for parents and other adults to provide their teenager or young adult appropriate information about the situation and include them in decision making where appropriate.

There are other losses which may affect a young person's hopes and dreams for the future. A breakup of a significant relationship (see Question 19) can also lead to grief and a loss of dreams regarding the hoped-for future of the couple. Suffering a sexual assault (see Question 17) will lead to intense grief and a variety of losses. Because of grief around the assault, changes in a young person's outlook on life can arise and may negatively affect the way they see themselves and their future. Often, accompanying feelings of sadness and depression can affect grades or job performance.

Even though the loss of hopes and dreams may be secondary to another loss, typical grief feelings will arise and may intensify other emotions arising from the primary loss. In some cases, the grief can become difficult to handle and a teenager or young adult may experience more serious emotional and psychological distress and/or deal with depression or prolonged complicated grief (see Questions 5 and 27).

The emotions and reactions associated with the loss of hopes and dreams can appear again, even after a young person deals with these feelings in positive ways. Milestone events, like same aged friends graduating from college, or a close friend getting married or experiencing a happy relationship, or seeing former teammates win a championship, can bring up feelings of loss again. These feelings are natural and will hopefully be dealt with in constructive ways. However, if such milestone events lead to deepened and more prolonged grief, it's important for the teenager or young adult to seek help from bereavement or mental health professionals.

Other than suggestions already made, there are other possibilities for coping with the loss of hopes and dreams. The most important step is to find those who will be a support, who will understand, listen, and encourage. Hopefully, parents or other trusted adults, like teachers, school counselors, or a therapist, can provide help and a listening ear. If the loss of hopes is secondary to another, it may be helpful to deal with the primary loss first, or at least come to understand the sources of the feelings and emotions that might emerge around the loss.

When dealing with the loss of hopes and dreams, it can be helpful to discover what the dream or aspiration truly means, or how the bereaved envisioned their wishes and goals were going to affect their life. It's also essential to deal with the grief emotions and to understand such feelings are normal and to be expected. Working toward letting go of one dream while creating another can be difficult, but is possible with the right support. Making new plans, sorting out possibilities, finding alternatives, seeking help where needed, and embracing a new direction are positive ways to cope and signs of strength and well-being.

Finding happiness and joy in life is a hope for most everyone. Discovering ways to journey through life while coping with disappointments and embracing hope, even when things do not work out, is an incredibly valuable life skill. Making new meaning and creating new paths is one of the goals of a healthy grief process, and imagining new hopes and dreams can be a part of the journey.

Experiencing Grief

21. How long does grief last?

A commonly held stereotype regarding grief is that it has a time limit, typically believed to be six months to a year. The grieving teenager may hear questions like "Why aren't you over that yet?" or "Are you *still* sad about Jenn's death?" Or the bereaved person may feel they should be "over it by now" even though the loss happened just a year or two ago. But, grief does not have a time limit. Grief is a unique experience for each person who suffers a loss. Bereaved people not only grieve differently, they also take differing amounts of time to deal with the emotions, thoughts, and changes that may accompany loss. In other words, grief happens at its own pace. It may be the case that a teenager adapts quickly while another young adult will take two or three years to accept and adjust to the loss. The young person could adjust relatively quickly to the death in terms of day-to-day functioning, but still deal with bouts of sadness or anger or some other reaction at surprising moments, or be affected when there is a graduation or milestone. In short, some bereaved teenagers may adjust to the loss and return to familiar routines and interactions with relatively few difficulties, while others find healing and the courage to move on after a longer struggle.

It is normal to expect that a bereaved person will begin to adjust to a loss after a reasonable period of time and that the feelings and emotions that accompany grief will lessen in intensity. Even though reluctant to suggest any kind of timeline, a number of bereavement specialists have experienced a two- to three-year time frame for clients to find acceptance and begin to adapt to the loss. But, those who work with the bereaved are wary of giving a timetable, fearful that particular time frame will become a rule. It is generally recognized by experts in the field that an attempt to give a definitive time frame can actually be detrimental to adaptation and healing.

The timing of grief and the ability to cope with the loss often depends on several factors. First, the person who died and the closeness of the relationship or level of attachment are critical influences (see Question 3). The death of a parent or sibling may have a greater impact on various levels than the death of a known, but distant cousin or uncle. A close friend's death may be more difficult to cope with than that of a relative (see Question 10). The way a person dies can also affect the timing of grief. For example, unexpected, traumatic deaths will be more disorienting and a shock to a person's daily routines and worldview, which may affect the time needed to cope (see Questions 12 and 13). A long-term illness, especially if it affects the dying person's appearance, or their ability to walk, speak, feed themselves, or other functional capacities (e.g., as with Parkinson's, Alzheimer's, ALS, some forms of cancer) can be traumatic and deplete energies available when the person dies. Such an experience can also affect the period of time it takes the bereaved young person to cope with the loss. Another critical factor is the support system available (e.g., family, friends, professionals, other adults) and when the support is utilized by the bereaved young person. Funerals, memorial services, and other rituals can help to moderate and explore feelings, give expression to mourning, and find support from others. Consequently, participating in or helping to plan services and other rituals (when possible) can help the bereaved teenager to come to acceptance and find healing more rapidly. Other factors that can affect the timing of grief include the bereaved person's general capacity to cope; the age or developmental stage of a teenager or young adult (see Question 6); cultural and religious history, values, beliefs, and contexts (see Questions 37–39); concurrent or ongoing crises and stresses in a young person's life; and previous experience with death.

The impulse to specify a timeline for bereavement may involve perceiving grief as something to accomplish or endure. A timeline also implies a linear or predictable process. However, grief is fluid and changes, is unique to each person, and can be unpredictable. Though there are commonalities around tasks and emotions bereaved young people face when grieving, the process is not a step-by-step progression. A teenager may flow in and out of periods of grief and mourning, dealing with the pain when they are able, while dealing with day-today concerns. Even those who have accepted and adapted to the loss will still feel pangs of sadness and grief years later, and some who work with the bereaved believe that grief never ends, though it may change with time and certainly lessen in intensity. In other words, it is normal to miss your loved one or a close friend five, ten, or even forty years after the death. Your love for them does not die. A moving example of this experience comes from the life of Dr. Morrie Schwartz. Dr. Schwartz was a sociology professor at Brandeis University whose courageous struggle with amyotrophic lateral sclerosis (ALS) was documented on *Nightline* and in the book *Tuesdays with Morrie*, by Mitch Albom. On *Nightline*, Ted Koppel interviewed Morrie regarding his disease and the lessons he was learning while struggling with ALS. At one point in the interview, the conversation focused on the death of Morrie's mother when he was eight years old, a death that occurred seventy years before. As he was relating his story, Morrie began to tear up, became emotional, finding it difficult to speak—all normal signs of grief. Ted Koppel was taken aback, and questioned Morrie about his reaction. Dr. Schwartz responded that the feelings can stay with you through the years. Other feelings, events, and issues were a part of the reaction as well, all triggered by connecting with the pain suffered seventy years before. However, Morrie shared that the tears strengthened him and further comments suggested that dealing with the ongoing grief was a help as he faced dying from ALS.

For Morrie, a letter from a teacher led to his experiencing feelings of grief connected to a death 70 years before. Other events can spark feelings of grief too, like anniversaries, birthdays, weddings, graduations, and other significant milestones or occasions. An offhand comment, an e-mail from a loved one or friend, a walk in a place important to the person who died, looking through photos and many other activities can bring up strong feelings associated with a significant loss, even if the loss happened a considerable time ago. As long as the intensity of grief diminishes or eases over time, or is relatively uniform and does not cause deeper anxiety or depression, such episodes are normal. However, if a few years after the death a person's sadness or depression or other reactions deepen and become more intense, or if the bereaved is unable to cope with day-to-day functioning, then help will definitely be needed. The intensity and frequency of some responses are critical signs of deeper issues and will likely require the help of mental health professionals (see Questions 27 and 29). In most cases, though, the ability to cry, grieve, and mourn, even years later, is normal and can be a healthy response to a deep and abiding memory, connection, or sorrow. As with Dr. Schwartz, such reactions can also be a source of strength.

22. I need some time off to deal with the shock and pain. Can I get time off from school? From work? What kind of time can I expect?

A significant loss, especially the death of a family member or friend, is traumatic and often devastating. The first few days after the death are particularly trying and a time when emotions are overwhelming. Of course, one's sense of loss and the reactions that ensue do not disappear after a few days, but are understandably more intense immediately after the loss. Because life and emotions can be so chaotic, counselors, bereavement specialists, and others recognize and advocate for time off from work or school after the death of a family member or loved one. Doing so allows the bereaved time in those first moments to begin the process of grief as well as deal with other practical issues that arise because of the loss. Those who work directly with grieving people would suggest greater amounts of time, but societal demands in the United States temper the number of days off a person can expect after such a loss.

School bereavement policies for students are more generous than those in business and many other settings, though there may be limitations specific to location. Nonetheless, policies in educational institutions are typically flexible, which allows the leave to be shaped to specific needs and circumstances of the student.

In secondary schools, time off regarding bereavement is typically found in the attendance policies of a school district or particular school. Although school districts have guidelines, some give freedom to individual schools to tweak policies within reasonable limits. The policies are varied among school districts, even those within close proximity. Some offer specifics regarding bereavement and other reasons for excused absence, while others indicate excused absences for reasons other than medical concerns need to be negotiated with the school or administrator handling attendance issues. The policies are fairly standard in requiring a note for the absence to be turned in within three days. However, if circumstances allow, notification of an absence for a death in the family, and appropriate arrangements for dealing with schoolwork can be made before the student returns to school.

Some policies mention that a student can miss up to five days for a death in the immediate family, while others do not give specifics. Most attendance policies seem flexible, as long as the number of days do not exceed guidelines concerning the allowable number of excused absences in a semester or year. There also seems to be latitude regarding absences for deaths of friends or other close relatives. Some teachers and administrators have allowed a day's or two days absence for other losses, like a close family pet. Schoolwork can be made up, but conversation needs to happen with particular teachers regarding the assignments and the length of time allowed to make up missed work or exams. In making decisions, teachers and administrators must balance a concern for the emotional well-being of the student with attention to educational needs and requirements for the bereaved teenager. Since many adults have dealt with loss and grief, teachers and administrators often act in empathetic and compassionate ways when a student suffers loss. Some schools have counselors that can help the bereaved teenager navigate their return to school and educational concerns and should be notified in the case of a death or major loss. Some school districts list bereavement services available in the community as well. Usually, the principal, school administrator, or attendance officer administers the polices and makes final decisions regarding absences and make up work, typically with consultation with teachers.

The bereavement policies of colleges and universities are similar to one another, though there are certainly variances between schools. Most higher education institutions understand that loss and the circumstances around the death of a loved one or someone special will be different from case to case, as will the reaction of the student affected by the loss. School staff and faculty are also aware that loss is tragic and can have a profound effect on the student's short-term and long-term academic progress as well as their emotional, spiritual, and physical well-being. The care of the student is a clearly stated core value of most universities and colleges, and their bereavement policies reflect such values.

Colleges and universities typically allow five weekdays or a week of excused absence after the death of an immediate family member or simply a member of the family. Most schools define "family member" rather broadly, and can include uncles, aunts, in-laws, step-relatives, and first cousins. Some will allow for excused absences when there is a death of someone special like a friend, family friend, or distant relative, but these cases must be approved by the appropriate office or department that handles bereavement issues. Additional days of excused absence may be negotiated in special circumstances. It is also possible for students to take a semester's leave of absence when a loved one dies, but there is a separate process to follow in these instances. Questions considered when determining time include, but are not limited to: "Who passed away?," "Was the death sudden?," "How far must the student travel?," and "What other family members are able to help with the arrangements?" The grief reactions of the student, and the change in circumstances (financial, family, living) are also strong factors regarding decisions made. Most policies require documentation at some point, such as a death certificate or the funeral program.

Bereavement policies for students are often administrated by the Academic Dean's office, though some schools have a Division of Student Affairs or Office of Student Success that will manage bereavement needs. Typically, the offices will notify faculty, advisors, and academic staff when a student takes leave after the death of a loved one or friend. Some will help the student negotiate extensions, incompletes, withdrawal from a particular class, or even withdrawal from the university. When a student takes more time than the standard bereavement leave, the student's individual instructors will often be involved when negotiating completion of classes and course requirements.

Time off from employment is more varied and not typically as generous as educational institutions. Bereavement leave offered by businesses is considered a benevolence since there are no federal laws that require employers to offer time off for bereavement. In fact, Oregon is the only state that has legally mandated bereavement time for employees, though the law does not apply to all companies or employers. A recent bill in New York that would have mandated employers to offer up to twelve weeks of bereavement leave was passed by the legislature, but vetoed by the governor due to concerns about cost to businesses as well as lack of specificity in the bill. Since there is no legal mandate nationally, statewide or locally, bereavement policies for businesses vary widely, and it is best to consult the particular business, human resources department, personnel manual or other resource that designate the benefit policies of the company.

Many businesses offer three to five days bereavement leave which will sometimes include the funeral, or can be days in addition to attending the funeral. The bereavement leave can be paid or unpaid. The time off will be dependent on the relationship to the deceased, with longer amounts of time given for immediate family members. In the case of businesses, "immediate family member" is more narrowly defined than for universities and colleges. Often, the immediate family member is a parent, sibling, spouse, child, stepparent, or stepchild. Bereavement leave can also be given for the death of other family members, but likely for shorter periods of time. Some companies may allow time off for the death of a friend or more distant relative, but again depends on the wording and content of bereavement policies or the decision of the business owner or human resources manager. Care is typically taken to make sure the policies are uniformly applied. If there are other issues that accompany the loss, such as care for surviving family members, the need for the employee to seek extensive grief counseling or to deal with health-related problems associated with the loss, the employee may be eligible for extended time off under the Family Medical Leave Act (FMLA). This provision allows for up to twelve weeks of unpaid, job protected time off. However, the FMLA has particular criteria regarding employers that qualify to offer time off under the FMLA, as well as guidelines for employees regarding eligibility for the benefit. These guidelines and criteria can be found at the U.S. Department of Labor website (dol.gov).

Although bereavement benefits are more likely for a full-time, permanent hire, some businesses offer bereavement time for part-time workers as well. Teenagers and young adults who work seasonal jobs may find employers to be more restrictive concerning bereavement time. Recent lawsuits and other pressures have caused larger businesses to expand, or consider expanding bereavement leave policies, especially for part-time or hourly workers. Advocates continue to work to expand benefits for all workers regarding bereavement benefits.

23. Is it okay to be angry?

Based on Kübler-Ross's writings and observations, anger was viewed early on in bereavement work as one of the stages of grief, and thus a typical response of those experiencing loss (see Question 2). Even so, societal and individual views about anger lead some to wonder if being angry is OK, or to what extent and for how long such a feeling is acceptable when dealing with loss. Some feel that such responses are unacceptable or feel threatened and confused when the source of anger is elusive or misunderstood. Others may believe that expressing anger is not helpful. Still others feel like expressing anger, especially at the person who died, is akin to speaking ill of the dead or disrespecting their memory, and thus taboo. Often anger is linked with hate, resentment, rage, jealousy, bitterness, and other similar feelings, which makes it difficult for the bereaved to feel okay when angry emotions arise. However, when dealt with in healthy ways, anger can be of help to the grieving person.

Some teenagers and young adults may wonder why they become angry when they suffer a loss; they may also be afraid of these feelings. Those who work with persons experiencing grief or do research around loss acknowledge that anger emerges among the bereaved for various reasons and is directed at various people and places. Anger often arises when a person—teenager, young adult, or older adult—experiences deepening frustration over a situation, or feels a lack of control regarding life circumstances. When there is a threat or harm, the fight or flight response often occurs accompanied by anger and fear. Anger can also arise when young people struggle with deep emotional pain or when coping with anguish and heartache that emerges around loss. A person who is severely disappointed because the way life is turning out, or believe life circumstances are unfair, can also develop feelings of resentment. Some experience irritation and other anger-like emotions when looking to restore something that has been lost but are unable to do so.

Anger can be directed at a variety of people and organizations. Depending on the illness or manner of death for a loved one, a bereaved young person may become outraged at an uncaring medical complex, hospitals, insurance companies, or anyone in businesses or organizations related to the death of their loved one or friend. Individual physicians may be blamed for not doing enough to prevent the death, or a social worker for failing to organize appropriate care. Some may be angry at funeral directors, clergy, or others who may be perceived as co-conspirators around death and loss, or for failing to provide high enough levels of attentiveness to those suffering loss. Family members can be the object of a teenager's ire when they feel the truth was not told about their loved one's condition or disease. A young person may be aggravated at friends, family, or acquaintances if they believe someone did not care deeply enough for the family member or friend that died. Anger can emerge around the will and estate of the deceased, or of the pettiness and arguments that can often arise when someone dies.

Some may feel a growing irritation with the deceased, wondering "how could they leave me?" or frustrated that their loved one did not prepare well enough and left the family in difficult circumstances. The grieving teenager may be upset their loved one did not take care of themselves well enough or pay attention to clear signs of health issues. A teenager or young adult might experience deep feelings of resentment at a parent or adult family member who has died for things previously said or done that were hurtful, harmful, or mean spirited.

For some bereaved young people, the anger may be directed more at themselves, especially if there are guilt feelings around their treatment of their deceased loved one. If the teenager believes they could have done something to prevent the death, or did something that contributed to the decline of their loved one, then guilt and anger can certainly arise. Since anger often accompanies bereavement, the young person may feel uncomfortable being angry with others and will turn the anger inward.

God, a higher power, or the life force of the universe may also be the target of irritation and rage. If a teenager believes death is a punishment, then resentment can certainly arise at the divine for being mean or callous. A young person may imagine God has power over the details of life and death and question why the divine failed to intervene on behalf of their loved one. Or a young person may wonder why God was not faithful to their loved one who had been so faithful to God. A bereaved person may also feel abandoned by a higher being or the universe itself, feeling deserted and alone resulting in feelings of anguish and resentment. Hebrew and Christian scripture is rife with examples of persons being angry or irritated with God, like Job, Jonah, some writers of the Psalms, and even Jesus ("Why have you forsaken me?").

Considering societal attitudes and the potential sources and targets of anger, is it even possible to view this emotion as something good or helpful? When dealt with in healthy ways, bereavement professionals and researchers would say yes. Anger is often a natural response to concerns, events, or loss. George Bonanno (in the *Other Side of Sadness*) and other bereavement experts say that anger likely evolved as an emotional response to harm in general, but also developed as a response to threats, painful situations, being cheated, demeaned, and marginalized. When a person perceives a threat or feels they are being harmed, there are physiological and other responses that help focus thoughts and resources needed to engage the threat, find ways to survive or figure out how to defend one's self. Anger is often noticeable in facial expressions as well and is a signal to others who are a threat, or to those who can help. When a young person is angry, especially in measured ways, it can open them to a sense of courage to handle issues and circumstances in a proactive way. It may help the bereaved teenager to deal with insensitive friends, the medical bureaucracy, or challenging family dynamics. It may be that a young person simply needs to express frustration or irritation. Even anger at God or a higher power indicates that such a relationship is valued and important and a potential source of inner strength.

The bereaved young person should not be judged for their anger in light of the circumstances. Even though such feelings can cause a person to be less trusting and more careful, they can also lead to a new and deeper relationship or different ways of perceiving the world or universe. For example, in *A Grief Observed*, C. S. Lewis rails against God in anger, and feels abandoned by God after the death of his wife, Joy. This is probably surprising for many to hear of such responses from a well-known theologian and person of faith. However, his honest reactions, spiritual struggles, and the deeper relationship with God that emerged for him have been an inspiration to others who have suffered loss.

However, there are times when angry feelings can be a cause for concern. Excessive and prolonged outbursts can be harmful and hurtful to oneself and others. When anger is too explosive, it may get in the way of positive effects, cause the bereaved to lose focus and attention on what matters or is needed, or spiral into other harmful emotional or physiological responses. Excessive and prolonged anger can get in the way of adapting to the loss or a return to normal functioning and life. Sigmund Freud is credited with saying that "anger turned inward is depression." Although depression cannot be described in such simplistic terms, anger left to fester and turned inward can lead to toxic guilt, low self-esteem and bitterness. It can also lead to more harmful psychological effects, including suicidal thoughts or action. Denying anger, setting it aside, or refusing to express anger in healthy ways is also problematic. It can disrupt needed emotional responses and keep the bereaved from confronting threats or other feelings related to loss, which may lead to chronic or complicated grief.

Since anger may indeed emerge as one grieves, it's important for teenagers and young adults to find healthy outlets and ways to express such feelings. As with grief in general, it's good to have a strong support system. A good support person or group that can listen to and handle strong emotions, especially anger or outbursts is critical. Such helpers are those who can hear the feelings without judgment or a need to argue or defend. Hopefully, the supportive person can offer comfort and encouragement, though simply listening without judgment can be an important balm for the bereaved teenager or young adult.

Apart from trusted family members, friends, or support groups, bereavement counselors, therapists, psychologists, and licensed mental health professionals can also be helpful. A skilled therapist or counselor will typically work to uncover the anger and its sources in an indirect way. Instead of asking, "Why are you so angry?" which may sound dismissive, judgmental and harsh, the counselor may say "what do you miss about your friend?" or, "does the death of your father make you feel like life is unfair?" Reframing the questions can provide a safe way for meaningful exploration of feelings.

Helpful methods for coping with angry feelings and related emotions include talking about positive aspects of the one who has died, sharing meaningful stories, or speaking about positive feelings and experiences related to the deceased. Doing so offers balance and a chance to discover paths of healing and transformation. Physical activity, journaling, and other activities may help the young person cope with anger as well.

What may be most helpful, though, is understanding that anger may be needed in the moment as a way to inspire the bereaved young person, give them a sense that there are things to do, alert them to other feelings and attitudes at the heart of their distress, and give them courage to confront offenses and injustices.

24. Someone close to me is dying and I'm having a hard time being upbeat and positive for them. Is that okay?

Tyler was sixteen when his grandmother was diagnosed with cancer. He and his grandmother were close. She had been relatively independent, but when they found her cancer was not responding to therapies, Tyler's parents brought his grandmother to live with them. She first received palliative care, but as the illness advanced Tyler's grandmother began hospice care (see Question 34 and Glossary). The family included him in the caregiving and kept him informed about her illness and health. While she lived with the family, Tyler watched favorite television shows with his grandmother and would often have long talks with her. As her disease progressed, he continued staying close, participating in activities she felt strong enough to do. He would bring her favorite ice cream and sometimes read to her. Tyler remained upbeat around his grandmother and felt energized by being able to help out. After a little over a year of his grandmother living with the family, Tyler began to feel different, even depressed, though nothing had changed in his relationship with his grandmother or his feelings about helping her. He was finding it more difficult to feel upbeat and positive. He could not shake thoughts about her death and how much he would miss her. "What's wrong with me?" he would think, not wanting such thoughts to interrupt the good times he was having with his grandmother. He was also missing important events with friends. The ambiguous feelings he was experiencing made it difficult for Tyler to have the energy to spend more time with his grandmother and also affected his sleep and schoolwork. Thankfully, the hospice team noticed Tyler's distress and helped facilitate family conversations around his and their feelings.

When a loved one or someone close to you is dying or has been diag-nosed with a life-limiting illness, it is normal to begin experiencing loss and grief even though they are still alive. Those who research bereavement or who work with the bereaved have named these feelings *anticipatory grief*. The extent to which someone encounters and are affected by these feelings depends on a number of factors, such as the depth of relationship a teenager or young adult has with the person who is dying, the young person's coping abilities, the circumstances around the life-limiting illness and the developmental situation of the young person. Studies have been mixed regarding anticipatory grief and whether it moderates the pain of loss after the person has died, although experiencing grief earlier on may allow the survivor to cope better, or to experience quicker access to adaptive capabilities after their loved one or close friend has died.

Many of the reactions a teenager or young adult may feel with anticipatory grief is much like that of typical bereavement responses. Besides the issues mentioned in Tyler's case, young people can feel things like sadness, anger, loneliness, and may find themselves withdrawing at times from family or family discussions. Teenagers and young adults may experience depression, anxiety, and low self-esteem as well, especially if the loved one dying is a parent or parent figure. Often it is difficult to talk with friends and peers, feeling that no one can or does understand. It's also difficult, when the time comes, to say goodbye, or to say the things you really want to say. If, like Tyler, a teenager or young adult begins to feel like their sadness is getting in the way of day-to-day relationships, guilt may arise over such feelings. Some teenagers and young adults, like many adults, may feel a little resentful or frustrated around the disruptions that are happening in one's "normal" life.

Along with these feelings, other challenges associated with anticipatory grief may arise, especially when a loved one is dying. For example, a young person may begin thinking more about their own mortality, or become worried that other persons close to them may become sick. Family routines will definitely change, and at times a teenager or young adult may take on different roles, such as caring for younger siblings, or even acting as the adult if a parent is unable to cope. If hospice is involved, relative strangers will be entering the home frequently and medical equipment and medications needed for the care of loved ones will become commonplace. Also, healthy experiences important for growth and maturity, like the need to separate emotionally from the family and connect more with peers, can be disrupted. In these cases, resentment can build, or the family may misunderstand the craving for independence as selfish. All of these issues may lead to feelings that are typical of someone grieving and mourning loss.

There are a number of reactions that can occur and each young person's experience of anticipatory grief will be unique to their life and circumstances. Whatever the responses may be, it's important to deal with the feelings and reactions so that healthy grief and relationships may endure. Sorting out emotions, thoughts, and concerns can help the young person cope in better ways, and may help with healing and adapting after a loved one or close friend has died. It's critical to seek out a support system, of those like trusted family members or friends, a guidance counselor, or grief counselor. If hospice is involved, members of the hospice team can be a nonthreatening person with distance from the family that can allow for the expression of open and honest feelings. It may also be important to be informed about a loved one's illness and be included in the care. Writing in a journal, making a memory book with you loved one who is dying, creating a website for the family as well as other ways to express your feelings, or take a breath, are also essential. A teenager and young adult can also be a great support for their loved one by giving them permission to express their feelings. Remember to say "I love you," give your loved one hugs, listen and ask questions, be honest and kind, find out how they're feeling, and be prepared for tears and strong emotions if up to the task. These and other ways of coping and being in relationship with a loved one who is dying are helpful and healthy ways of coping with anticipatory grief.

Hopefully, others will be looking out for the well-being of a young person as they are dealing with anticipatory grief. Accepting unpredictable feelings, honoring the young person's need to know, offering information in appropriate ways, including the teenager or young adult in conversations and care, or creating space for a time out or time with friends are all ways to help. If these ways of helping are not happening, the young person may need to ask for what they need.

25. What do I do with my feelings of guilt and shame?

Guilt, regret or shame, along with feelings like sadness and anger, happen on a frequent basis for those who have suffered loss. The bereaved may say things like, "I wish I hadn't fought with my father the day before he died," or "if I would have been paying attention, this would not have happened." Statements that begin with "I wish . . .," "if only . . .," "I should have . . ." are usually ones that describe why a teenager or young adult might feel guilt or regret.

There are many other circumstances that can lead to these feelings when a young person suffers a significant loss. For instance, a young person and their family may feel relief after a loved one suffering from a long-term illness dies (see Questions 3 and 26), or a teenager may be upset and feel guilty if they were not present when a loved one died. Perhaps a young adult, because of other responsibilities for school and work, felt they did not offer enough support and care, or a teenager may experience guilt feelings because they believe they could have been more helpful to a friend who died by suicide. Sometimes a young person might blame themselves for a death, or they may feel guilty that their feelings of sadness or loss are not intense enough. Survivor's guilt, not being kind enough, failing to do something or say something, having a strained relationship with the person who died, and many other situations and circumstances can lead to deep feelings of guilt, regret, and even shame.

Though guilt, regret, and shame are different many may use the terms interchangeably. But, it's important to distinguish these feelings from one another, because they arise from different circumstances and the approaches for dealing with them effectively may differ.

In her 2012 book *Daring Greatly*, Brené Brown says guilt arises when we do something that does not match up with our values, or our sense of right and wrong. Usually, guilt can motivate us to make a change and can be a helpful emotion that leads to remorse, making an apology, or making amends. Brown says that shame, on the other hand, "is the intensely painful feeling or experience of believing we are flawed and therefore unworthy of love and belonging." Guilt comes from an internal assessment and struggle. Shame is usually something we feel because a community, group or person has made us feel that way. Whereas guilt is about doing or saying something bad, shame is the feeling that one is bad. For Brown and others, shame is destructive and has little redeeming value, while coping with guilt in healthy ways can lead to positive outcomes and healing.

Regret often results when something happens we wish we could change or prevent, or that turns out differently than we had hoped, or wishing we had said or done something different. Issues around regret do not violate one's conscience, though it may still be painful or distressing. For example, a young person may be upset that a close grandparent who suffered a long illness died while they were at school. Though there may be feelings of deep pain and sorrow for not being there with their loved one, there was nothing the teenager or anyone else could have done to predict the timing of death.

Societal and cultural norms may affect how a person deals with guilt, regret, and shame. Though there may be differences, it's vitally important to deal with guilt and shame because if left unattended they can evolve into anger, bitterness, and fear. Unresolved guilt, regret, or shame can also affect our relationships with others, a higher power, or our interaction with the world. Dealing with these emotions in a healthy way is important for one's ability to cope, seek meaning and purpose, and overall well-being.

As with other aspects of bereavement a good support network, or having someone trusted to talk with, is critical for dealing with guilt or regret. Often the bereaved may hear statements that attempt to explain away the guilt, like "oh, you shouldn't feel that way," or "there's nothing you could have done." Such statements are dismissive and may keep the bereaved teenager from expressing their deepest feelings. It's important, then, to find those who can be calm and nonjudgmental when the bereaved shares painful moments and concerns. Doing so allows the person grieving to embrace the guilt or regret and explore avenues for healing.

Although grief, regret, and shame are different, a bereaved young person or adult experiencing pangs of guilt may not stop to discern whether their feeling is one or the other. However, if the person in grief is able to find space and support to explore such feelings, knowing the differences can be helpful in discerning the best ways to cope and deal with emotions. Usually, the best way to deal with guilt is forgiveness, whether the bereaved needs to forgive themselves or find other ways for forgiveness to take place. Making amends can also be a part of the process as is making apologies. Writing a letter to the deceased is often a way to explore guilt feelings and remedies. The way to deal with shame is through empathy and reframing. Often the bereaved will need to be in conversation with someone who can identify with their pain, have their back, and help the grieving person understand such feelings arise from the judgmental attitude of others or society. Letting go of shame, or reframing the feelings in a more beneficial way, is essential. For regret the grieving young person may need to find a way to learn from the experience, or to understand that circumstances are often out of their control, or to find a way to accept the circumstances as they are and move to a place of healing.

Oftentimes, guilt feelings come from irrational thoughts of the bereaved about the death and their role in it, or regarding their relationship with the person who died. It's helpful for the grieving young person to find someone to help them do a reality check and examine facts and frame of reference. In the case that legitimate guilt exists, the person helping the bereaved needs to be honest and help them explore interventions and help. Unattended guilt and shame can also lead to complicated grief (see Question 27). If a grieving young person is able to cope effectively with guilt, regret, and shame their experience can help others, or they may be moved to do something positive stemming from what they have learned.

Feelings of guilt are a normal reaction to loss, but should be dealt with head on and with the help of trusted friends and family. There are times, though, when these feelings can lead to deeper issues and forms of grief. In some cases, the guilt can evolve into a more general sense of guilt characteristic of major depression. When feelings of guilt or shame are present in these ways, it is critical to be in touch with therapists and bereavement specialists (see Questions 5, 27, and 34).

26. Are there ever positive emotions associated with grief?

Discussion about grief responses typically focus on the more challenging and painful emotions regarding loss, like sadness and anger. This is not surprising since early writings around grief and loss heavily influenced the conversation around bereavement and the feelings and issues that usually emerged. Sigmund Freud's essay "Mourning and Melancholia" and Elisabeth Kübler-Ross's *On Death and Dying* focused attention on reactions like sadness, separation, denial, anger, and depression. Many others who worked with the bereaved or studied grief responses also focused on the difficult feelings around loss (see Question 3). Even though sadness in particular is common for those experiencing loss, research in the last fifteen to twenty years has shown the importance of positive emotions and memories in the grieving process. Studies examining bereavement have found that persons experiencing loss typically have better long-term adjustment and coping if they express positive emotions early in the grief process.

It's not uncommon for teenagers and young adults to share stories about the person who died when gathering with friends or family, or even at a funeral or memorial service. Many a tale or memory of a loved one or friend brings a smile to the face or elicits laughter. Smiling and genuine laughter not only reveal depths of gratitude and good feelings about the deceased, but also have positive effects on the person who has suffered loss and those around them. Studies have shown that those who laugh and smile more often are typically healthier emotionally and physically in general, and the same is true for those who are bereaved. Laughter and smiling also provide a chance to take a break from the sadness one feels or the pain that accompanies loss. Even if temporary, such breathing space has healthy consequences for the bereaved. The oscillation between sadness and laughter or painful feelings and positive memories is a normal part of the grieving process. Researchers have noted that this wave-like movement of emotions and thoughts is more typical of the grief process than stages or steps (see Question 3) and helps the person experiencing bereavement to better cope with the loss.

Another positive feeling connected to loss is relief. It is understandable that a teenager and their family may experience such a feeling when a loved one dies after a long and painful illness (see Question 24). Caregiving at any level for a loved one who has been bedridden and faced multiple challenges as they die takes a toll physically and emotionally. Depending on the relationship with the person who has died, the teenager may feel a deep sadness, but may also be glad their ill grandparent or family member has found release from physical and emotional suffering.

Teenage and young adult years are full of changes and development on many levels (see Question 6). Although care and attention are rightly focused on a loved one who is dying, a young person and their family often feel their life has been put on hold, or feel their concerns and challenges are unimportant. When a family member dies after a long illness, obligations and commitments shift and there may be a sense of relief. A feeling of relief may also occur when the relationship between a teenager/young adult and the person who died was strained or harmful to the young person. In these instances, the death may open new doors and possibilities, and the quality of life for the young person and other family members may improve.

Relief may understandably lead to feelings of guilt. A teenager or young adult may believe positive emotions are a betrayal, or may feel guilty because they think the help and care they provided was inadequate. A young person may be upset with themselves if the relationship with the deceased was strained, or if they did something to disappoint their loved one. There are many reasons a teenager or young adult may feel guilt or regret when they feel relieved after a death, but relief can actually be a critical step in the healing process. Such an emotion offers a chance to cope in healthy ways and may open the door for gratitude. Being able to spend time with their grandparent, uncle, or other family member, and offer them love and companionship as they are dying, can be seen as a gift, though such feelings may arise after dealing with the shock and sadness that accompanies loss.

Studies show that those who are able to express positive emotions during periods of grief adjust better and are more able to find healing. Though studies do not make the link between positive emotions during bereavement and developing positive meaning in life, it makes sense that better coping and healing can lead to finding meaning and greater purpose. Many times, families become closer and more supportive when they help a loved one during a long-term illness, or when they face a tragic loss together. The teenager or young adult may become more mature and self-confident due to the way they handled difficult circumstances with humor and grace, or because they volunteered to take on more responsibility during the illness of a relative or friend. Though the death of a loved one or friend is not the way a young person or anyone would want to learn life lessons, dealing with death and loss in positive ways increases the chance for deeper meaningful relationships and a greater appreciation for life.

27. What is complicated grief? Isn't all grief complicated?

Grief reactions can be rather intense, especially in the first days and weeks after a significant loss. They can look and feel overwhelming, cause the bereaved to lose their bearings, bring about questions around worldview and one's identity, and lead to behaviors that are uncharacteristic for the bereaved. However, most persons who suffer loss are able to navigate the terrain of grief in relatively healthy ways and are able to find ways to cope, adapt, and find new meaning. There are others, though, who struggle with loss, especially with the death of someone close or because of some other traumatic event. When acute grief becomes prolonged and accompanied by phobic, irrational, and obsessive thoughts and behaviors, then the grieving process is certainly far more complex and problematic. In these cases, the bereaved may suffer from what is known as complicated grief disorder (CGD) or prolonged grief disorder (PGD).

Complicated grief is a relatively new concept in the field of bereavement. Though the definition of this phenomenon is somewhat consistent among major researchers, there are no standard diagnostic tools or measurable criteria accepted at present. However, consensus is quickly emerging and an official designation in authoritative resources like the *Diagnostic and Statistical Manual of Mental Disorders* (DSM) may be available in the very near future. Current research suggests that 10 percent of bereaved persons suffer from complicated or prolonged grief. Using recent data about the number of deaths in the United States per year and the persons affected by each death, it's estimated that 500,000 to two million persons will go through some form of CGD annually.

Complicated or prolonged grief is understood as a disorder or syndrome that hinders and inhibits adaptation and healing. Although CGD/PGD is not an anxiety disorder, type of depression, or a form of PTSD, it can be related to these, and like the other disorders requires diagnosis and treatment. It differs from normal grief in that grief reactions are prolonged, intense, and accompanied by disabling emotional, mental, and behavioral responses. A common reaction that helps identify CGD/PGD is the presence of an obsessive focus on the loss, or a deep yearning, pining or longing for the deceased. In *The Other Side of Sadness*, George Bonanno asserts that for those suffering from prolonged grief "memories [of the deceased] fester and sour. They become, literally, haunting." The person suffering from complicated grief also becomes fixated on obsessive thoughts and emotions. Even when positive thoughts or emotions are present, they are hijacked by negative ones. Life loses meaning in reference to the loss, and as a result, the bereaved often experiences a muddled or profound loss of identity.

Other thoughts, emotions, and behaviors signal prolonged grief as well. Often the person avoids family and friends and reminders of their loss. If this occurs, the bereaved can become isolated, which in turn can affect the severity of CGD/PGD. This is a special concern for teenagers and young adults, since loss typically affects the way they interact with friends and family that would typically be supportive. On the other hand, the person suffering from prolonged grief can be consumed with finding items that remind them of their deceased loved one and may even imagine the deceased will miraculously return or believe they see the person that died. The one suffering from CGD can also obsess on the safety of other loved ones or worry incessantly about their ability to manage and cope with life. Intense feelings of guilt, anger, or bitterness may arise for prolonged and intense periods, or the bereaved may fixate on questions around the death or some aspect of the loss. There may be panic attacks, abuse of alcohol and drugs, or other emerging disorders (e.g., major depression, anxiety, PTSD).

Several factors have emerged important to diagnosing CGD/PGD. The severity of the grief reactions is a sign, and that responses are prolonged or have lasted longer than expected. Usually, the grief responses impede the ability to function or move toward coping and healing. Emerging consensus indicates the symptoms persist at least six months or longer before a diagnosis is made. Other signs include the bereaved speaking over and over about their loss, as if it just occurred, or when casual conversation about the deceased or a minor event brings about intense reactions. Someone may make radical life-changing decisions too soon, or the bereaved may refuse to move items from, or make changes to the room of the deceased after a reasonable time. A person suffering from CGD/PGD may develop acute fears around the circumstances of the death. Typically, a diagnosis may not result unless there are a cluster of thoughts, emotions, and behaviors that emerge for a prolonged period.

There are a few common risk factors or indicators that may trigger the development of CGD/PGD for young people and older adults alike.

For example, a complicated or dysfunctional relationship with the deceased, especially one in which the survivor was heavily dependent on their loved one, frequently leads to prolonged grief. The struggles around the loss of a child, or losing someone close to suicide or another severe traumatic event, or even around a failure to be present at the death can also progress into CGD/PGD. Suicide, mass shootings, fatal auto accidents involving friends, or circumstances around the death of parents, siblings, and friends are all risk indicators for developing complicated grief among bereaved teenagers and young adults. A history of anxiety and other mood disorders, unresolved issues with the deceased, and the occurrence of multiple losses at the same time or in close proximity can also lead to complicated grief responses. Another key risk factor is the absence of a support network.

Since PGD can look like other disorders, like major depression or PTSD, it is important to understand some of the differences, though diagnosis should be performed by a mental health and bereavement specialist. As with grief in general, those suffering CGD are preoccupied with feelings and thoughts focused on the deceased. With depression, the young person is usually focused on their own identity or will suffer from low self-esteem. For CGD a young person may feel intense guilt for letting down a parent who died, or may feel they could have prevented the death. For those suffering from depression, feelings of guilt are more general, as a state of being rather than focused on a particular relationship. With CGD, there is typically a strong yearning for the one who has died and a fanatic hope to connect with them in some way. Those dealing with depression do not exhibit the yearning tendencies of the person dealing with CGD. While thoughts are fixated on the deceased, those suffering complicated grief will avoid reminders about the actual death or loss. Even so, the person dealing with CGD can still retain a sense of self-worth and belief that the world is still good. Those suffering from depression typically feel unworthy and see the world as broken, and even unfixable.

CGD and PTSD are often conflated as well, since those with CGD often ruminate on images or memories of the deceased, or feel isolated from others, which are typical symptoms of PTSD. However, persons suffering with PTSD typically deal with intense fear for the safety or well-being of themselves or others, while the person with CGD focuses on sadness and yearning for the deceased. The person with PTSD exhibits an obsessive focus on the event that was traumatic, whereas the person with CGD focuses on the deceased and avoidance of memories around the circumstances of death. PTSD victims avoid dangerous situations, while the person with CGD may do whatever they can to feel close to the deceased.

There are a number of other factors and signs that distinguish these conditions as well. Proper diagnosis is critical then, since each condition is treated in different ways. However, though distinct, it's also possible that CGD, depression, and PTSD can overlap when a person is dealing with loss, especially if it is a traumatic death or the loss involves assault or some other trauma. So, appropriate diagnosis is essential so the bereaved young person can find the best way to cope and heal.

Although there are no universally accepted treatments for CGD/PGD, certain approaches are emerging as effective. Oftentimes certain problems or difficulties are at the root of the complicated bereavement. For example, a youth or young adult may have experienced abuse at the hands of a parent who has died, or the bereaved person's friend may have been the victim of a homicide or severely traumatic death. In these cases, the counselor will focus on resolving these issues before turning to other symptoms and causes. In general, the therapist will work to diagnose what issues are at the heart of the prolonged grief and then deal with each issue depending on severity and importance. Other researchers suggest the bereaved tell their story of the loss, how they experienced it, and what they perceive as affects. In telling the story, the areas of distress will emerge and be discerned by an experienced counselor. As with other forms of grief, it will be important for the bereaved to deal with thought patterns, behaviors and feelings that may be impeding their ability to cope and function. It will also be essential for the person dealing with CGD/PGD to make concrete plans and goals to begin moving toward a normal life. In the case of youth and young adults suffering prolonged grief, a counselor can help them to organize, prioritize, and bring structure to their life, especially when feeling overwhelmed.

28. I just don't want to deal with the sadness. What harm can that do?

Teenage and young adult years are a time to forge identity and develop a stronger sense of meaning, purpose, and values. Dealing with these concerns can be positive and life-giving, but can also be fraught with uncertainty, doubt and numerous life challenges. So, when a significant loss happens, it can be especially confusing and disturbing. It will also be disconcerting to deal with changes in daily routines of school and time with friends that often accompany the death of a someone close.

It's understandable as well to want to avoid feelings that are painful and distressing. Sadness and crying may also be difficult for friends and others to deal with, especially if grieving has gone on for some time. Showing intense emotion may also feel uncomfortable or isolating.

Since painful emotions are hard for some to deal with, the bereaved may feel pressure to set aside their sadness or tears so others will not abandon or criticize them. Or they are simply told to "control themselves" or "get it together." Often young people are expected to control their feelings or avoid expressing them so they can be there for their family and friends, or keep from adding to the pain others are feeling. The bereaved may also feel that setting aside or running away from the anguish and sorrow seems like the best thing to do, just to get by and deal with the day-to-day. Yet, avoiding the pain and refusing to deal with the sadness, especially for prolonged periods, can have detrimental effects. A young person might mask their pain by abusing substances like alcohol and drugs. Other feelings may arise that are harmful, like deep-seated anger, or the bereaved may find it difficult to cope and adapt and find new meaning in life.

Sadness is difficult, but it is an expected and important part of the grieving process. While such an emotion is challenging, it is an essential part of what it means to be human. Though many would like to avoid these feelings, sadness actually has positive functions that help us in our grief, and can also open the bereaved to growth and change. Since sadness can have positive functions and outcomes, dismissing or setting aside such feelings could inhibit or cut off healthy grieving. On the other hand, it's also true that sustained, prolonged sadness can be harmful, leading to further struggle and emotional difficulties. Given that sadness (or any intense emotion that arises as one grieves) has both positive and potentially harmful effects, it's important to embrace sadness in a supportive environment with people the young person trusts. It is also essential to be aware of the positive attributes of sadness for the grieving process.

Those who study emotional behavior have found that some emotions evolved over time to help human beings deal with particular threats or challenges. Like anger (see Question 23), sadness is one of the emotions important for human survival and adaptation. Sadness helps us to pay attention to critical aspects of our inner life as well as providing a way to react to the world and people around us.

One of the critical functions of sadness is to help focus the bereaved inward. There are some challenges, like the loss of a loved one, that require the young person to take a step back, martial needed emotional resources, and give space for deeper awareness and examining issues of meaning and identity. Researchers have found that sadness helps the bereaved to slow down, become more detail-oriented, increase decision-making capacity and focus on what's next. It also aides in helping the bereaved become more mindful of, or come to accept, what has been lost. Amidst the usual challenges and changes in a teenager's or young adult's life the function of sadness can be beneficial, allowing the young person a chance to take a pause, regroup, and begin focusing on the other changes and challenges that accompany grief. The opportunity to feel and reflect more deeply is particularly helpful when much of society is bent on moving on, keeping busy, or returning to normal activity.

Another helpful aspect of sadness involves what is communicated to those around us. We often show emotions to others in subtle and not so subtle ways, especially the most basic and important feelings like sadness. Our emotions are often shown facially, in the way we speak, or in our body language. Facial expressions that accompany sadness have also developed over time as a way to alert others to how we are feeling. While some may react in an unhelpful way, friends and family and others who are a young person's support will typically respond with sympathy, empathy, connection, and assistance.

Coping with sadness, especially for the grieving young person, can be burdensome if this feeling was present all the time. However, bereavement research has indicated that the grief process typically happens in a wave-like or oscillating fashion (see Question 3). One of the reasons for the oscillating nature of the grief process is that certain stresses and feelings cannot be sustained at the same intensity for prolonged periods. Otherwise, they may become harmful or destructive. Studies have found that a bereaved person's experience with sadness works in this wavelike manner, which allows the bereaved a chance to feel the pain and sadness, but at intervals so that it can do its work.

It is certainly possible to be overwhelmed by sadness and to let sorrow take over our everyday lives. Left unattended, there can be harmful outcomes. However, at these times, those who support the bereaved will often step in with a kind word or express sympathy. In these cases, the compassion and concern offered by others can be an antidote to the sadness that threatens to undermine steps toward healing.

However, it is possible for sadness to go on too long. If the teenager is too focused inward, or the young adult excessively preoccupied with aspects of the death or loss or the symptoms of the distress, or if other factors affect the ability to cope, harmful outcomes can result. For example, prolonged or continued sadness can evolve into complicated grief or depression (see Questions 5 and 27). At these moments, it is important for the young person to find professional help, or for their loved ones to offer support and encouragement for therapy.

When a young person (or anyone) suffers loss, especially major loss, it is inevitable that the sadness will come. In the midst of bereavement, especially early on, happiness or joy seems distant or impossible. A variety of emotions will arise as well, and grief can feel overwhelming. However, sadness is a crucial part of our humanity that allows us to cope and heal. The grief process itself is also a part of what it means to be human and a way to deal with profound loss in our lives. Though the challenges and changes that accompany bereavement are many, we are wired to face many of these challenges, adapt, and find new meaning. A healthy embrace of sadness, especially in appropriate doses, is one of the ways human beings are equipped in order to take a step back, reflect, and determine what to do next. Sadness also alerts others, especially trusted friends and family, that we need their compassion, encouragement, and help.

29. When should I be concerned? Can grief become a problem?

Grief is a natural process that occurs after loss, but sometimes emotions can become overwhelming or life circumstances associated with the loss can undermine security, expectations, and possibilities. The grief process can be more complex for teenagers and young adults since so many changes and challenges are happening at this time in their life. Young people often begin to separate emotionally and socially from family as a part of healthy growth and development, but doing so makes it difficult to turn to parents or other family members for help. Dealing with a loss is also isolating because some teenagers perceive that friends and family will be unable to commiserate or understand, again making it difficult to know where to turn.

In spite of these challenges, many teenagers and young adults are able to find the support they need to deal with the strong emotions and life changes that might occur. Like adults, they may exhibit resilience in the face of loss (see Question 36). Some young people may find the path more difficult and struggle with the loss for a time, but eventually be able to deal with the emotions and challenges that are associated with bereavement. However, others may become overwhelmed and lose their way, finding the pain of loss to difficult to bear and accept.

Since each bereaved person will grieve differently, it's not always easy to determine what kind of help a young person needs or if more significant intervention is required. In the first few months, inconsistent emotions and behavior is to be expected. But, as time goes on, it is important for those who care about a bereaved teenager or young adult to be attentive to their needs and if behaviors become concerning or alarming.

Typically, there are strong reactions to the loss or the young person may become apathetic or withdraw. In the first few months, such reactions are to be expected. But, if the bereaved continues to withdraw from family and friends, has trouble dealing with daily tasks, begins to struggle in profound ways with school, or decides to quit a once loved extracurricular activity, then it's important to show concern and see if the bereaved needs more significant help. Symptoms of depression (see Question 5), acute sleeping difficulties, physical issues that become more problematic, and a decline in self-esteem or interest in life are also signs that the bereaved is needing additional support. There are other behaviors that can be troubling as well, especially risk-taking behaviors like abuse of alcohol or drugs, sexual risks, or becoming antisocial or changing one's circle of friends. Suicidal tendencies or ideas are especially troubling and need immediate attention or intervention. Traumatic deaths, the suicide of a friend or relative, and associated issues of abuse or other trauma can also be risk factors for prolonged or complicated grief, depression, and other anxiety disorders (see Questions 5, 12, 13, and 27).

In the case that grief takes on these emotional and behavioral features, it is crucial that the grieving teenager or young adult be provided access to more comprehensive services and aide. Help can come in many forms (see Questions 31, 33, 34, and 35), but the most basic need is connection to a strong and trusted support system, which might include a trusted friend, family member, or other adult (teacher, guidance counselor, neighbor, clergy). It's important that these support persons be able to listen well and without judgment and allow the bereaved teenager or young adult space to talk or simply share time together. In some cases, the bereaved will need professional help, such as mental health counselors, bereavement specialists, or supervised support groups. If there is substance abuse, cutting, anxiety disorders, suicidal ideation, or other serious concerns, immediate help should be sought. Whatever the responses around loss may be, grief should never be experienced alone. Whether a teenager or young adult adapts well or faces more complicated grief, they are deserving of the attention, compassion, and care of others.

Finding Support When Coping with Grief

30. A person I knew at my high school/college just died, and many of us are feeling sad and uncertain. What do we do?

When there is a death of a student, teacher, or other staff at a high school or college, the loss can impact many at the school. Surely, grief and mourning are more intense for those closest to the person who dies. However, grief will have an effect on classmates, school groups and staff, acquaintances, and even the larger community. Whatever the situation, feelings of sadness, uncertainty, and other responses will arise. Although individuals will experience their own grief in unique ways, the loss will likely entail communal expressions of grief and mourning as well.

The movement toward healing and adapting to the loss is enhanced when your circle of friends or the community deals with the death openly and collectively. There are a number of public activities and events the bereaved can engage to aid communal grief and mourning. Candlelight vigils, either planned or spur-of-the-moment, are often helpful to groups and communities grieving loss. Vigils can be safe places for the expression of various emotions like sadness or anger. They also allow participants to remember together the person (or persons) who died by sharing stories about them. Vigils are also a place where community members express or hear messages of encouragement, hope, and possibly a call to action.

Vigils frequently have spiritual content or can simply be a silent gathering of those grieving the loss.

Sometimes creating makeshift memorials honoring the deceased can be an avenue for grief and healing. When the death is a result of a tragic event like an automobile accident, it's not unusual to see memorials appear at the site of the incident. Whatever the circumstances surrounding the death or the location of the site, memorial spots become a place for friends and acquaintances to visit to remember, cry, or place a symbol of their connection to the one who died.

There are other public events like funerals or prayer services, school assemblies, or already scheduled events that can help those who are grieving. After the shooting that killed ten students and teachers at Santa Fe High School in Houston, a game shortly after the tragedy involving the school's baseball team became a place to offer tribute to those who died and an occasion for mourning, solidarity, and hope. The students and players from Santa Fe High *and* the opposing team utilized other ways to express their grief; signs, t-shirts, armbands, and other items were used to offer messages honoring friends and teachers, as well as for inspiration and encouragement.

Hopefully, the administration at the high school or college is sensitive to losses that occur and prepare for times like these (see Question 22). Whether the death is of a friend or a family member, it's important for the loss to be acknowledged and accommodation given so the bereaved can have a chance to grieve and mourn. In the case of tragic losses or multiple deaths, schools and community leaders are often at the forefront planning memorials or other events. Making sure students are involved in the planning and participation, or giving freedom for students to organize their own events is crucial. After the mass shooting at Marjory Stoneman Douglas High School in Parkland, Florida, there were a number of vigils and events that allowed students and the community to vent their anger, share their sadness, offer stories and memories about friends and teachers, as well as a chance to speak words of hope and healing. The tragedy also led to several students becoming more engaged in public awareness and advocacy.

There are other actions that can be helpful as well. For example, gathering for a special dinner to honor and remember a friend, perhaps at their favorite restaurant, can be a way to celebrate their life and the friendship the group shares. The gathering of friends may happen more than once and even beyond the immediate weeks or months after the death. A once-a-year event, perhaps around the anniversary of a friend's death, is appropriate and can be deeply meaningful. Another way to honor and keep alive the memory of a friend who has died is to organize walks or other charity events to raise awareness and funds for things like cancer research or other organizations connected to the friend's death.

One of the most important things a group of friends or acquaintances can do is find time to be together. Finding time to simply enjoy normal routines or share memories and express feelings in an atmosphere of support and acceptance is vital. Talking about the loss, expressing fears, conveying the pain, or venting shared anger can all be helpful in the healing process. These encounters will not always be easy, and some friends may shy away from such an outward show of grief. Even so, relying on friends and others for support is invaluable as one deals with loss and grief.

31. How can I help a friend or someone else when they are grieving?

When a friend or someone close is grieving it is often difficult to know how to offer support. Many people feel they do not know what to say or do, and the anxiety over doing just the right thing sometimes prevents individuals from doing anything at all. However, when a friend is grieving they need a good support system of friends, family, and others willing to be part of the journey with them.

The most basic and important manner of helping is being present for a friend and listening—and when listening, really listen. Active listening means being attentive to the bereaved and not so worried about offering a response, unless your friend is truly asking for one. Active listening also entails trying to truly understand what the friend is saying as well as being attentive with compassion and a nonjudgmental attitude. When together with the bereaved, put away smart phones and avoid other distractions, unless you and the friend are using them for something specific or as part of your time together. Try not to ask too many questions and shy away from giving advice. Though it may feel uncomfortable, silence is okay and sometimes needed if the friend is struggling with difficult feelings and thoughts. A grieving friend needs a safe place to be themselves and work through their grief.

Being present is also a promise, a commitment to stick with the grieving friend, especially when there are uncomfortable moments. It's hard to express intense emotions in front of others, even with friends or family. So, being able to stay by someone when they are sad or angry is extremely valuable and lets the bereaved know their reactions are expected and a part of a healthy grieving process. Being present also conveys a sense of "normalcy." Normal routines and conversations are often helpful because it keeps the grieving person grounded. It's also important to avoid the impulse to fix things or make everything feel alright. Being there for a friend or someone who is grieving entails patient companionship as the bereaved journeys through difficult moments that are a part of grief and loss.

It's also important to understand that a grieving friend may act in unexpected ways. For example, a friend that's always joked around and been outgoing may withdraw and be introspective when dealing with a difficult loss. Remember that everyone deals with grief in different ways, and that the experience of loss can be affected by a variety of factors (e.g., who it was who died and the closeness of the relationship; cultural influences; family dynamics; personal coping skills).

When in conversation with a bereaved friend there are suggestions about what to say and not say (see Question 32 and other resources like The Dougy Center website, dougy.org). It's really important to avoid saying "I know how you feel," or things like "don't cry, it will be alright." Some comments like these may cut off conversation or make the friend believe their feelings do not matter or are insignificant. Instead, saying something like, "grief is different for everyone, how is it for you right now" may be more helpful. Or, crying along with the bereaved or offering a gesture of understanding and compassion is also helpful.

Sometimes, the person helping and walking with the bereaved has suffered a loss in the past and is familiar with grief and what accompanies bereavement. However, since everyone grieves in a unique way, equating one's own experiences or feelings with that of a bereaved friend can be unhelpful. Instead, let the friend know that you "get it" on some level, but also want to hear what they are going through and experiencing. It's also critical to give a friend that is grieving a free pass to say no, or "I don't want to talk about that right now." Try to be with the friend where they are and allow them to take the lead concerning where the conversation needs to go. Don't be afraid to talk about the deceased, and if you knew the person who died offering memories and stories or admiration can be helpful.

There are other helpful things one can do for someone who is grieving. Assisting the bereaved friend with homework is a way to offer critical support, since keeping up with school will be difficult. Perhaps helping out with a chore, watching a Netflix program, bringing over brownies, going to a game, or just hanging out can be beneficial. If invited, accompanying a friend in a special ritual or way to remember their loved one is meaningful and healing (like going to a favorite spot their uncle liked, going to the funeral or helping with a video of memories of their loved one). It's also helpful to remember the bereaved may be sad on birthdays or around the holidays. Sending a note through social media, or asking the person grieving to do something special on those days to remember the person who died can offer care and attention needed, while also honoring the friend's loved one.

Sometimes the feelings of the friend can be scary or overwhelming, or it seems like the bereaved is acting in ways that are harmful or distressing. If this is the case, it's important to share concerns with a trusted adult, whether a family member or school counselor or someone else who may have experience dealing with grief. If possible, suggest the friend talk to someone else, but if they refuse, it may be necessary to act. If your friend is in serious trouble emotionally, it's not a violation of their privacy to let someone else know you're concerned. Details of conversations do not need to be revealed, unless the friend plans to harm themselves or someone else. In the case of conversations around self-harm (especially suicide) or harming another, contact a hot line (see Directory of Resources) and speak with a trusted adult as soon as possible. If the threat of harm seems immediate, call 911. In dire circumstances, it's possible to be honest and assertive with the friend while letting them know you are not abandoning them.

Reaching out to someone who is grieving is an act of compassion and care. However, it's not an easy thing to do and can sometimes feel daunting. Attempts to reach out will be refused at times. However, the simple offer to be present and patiently listen can be exactly what a grieving friend may need, especially if others around them have withdrawn or lack the capacity to help. Being a part of another's journey and potential healing can be incredibly meaningful and deepen bonds of friendship. At the very least, it lets the person grieving know that there is someone who truly cares.

32. What should I say or avoid saying to someone who is grieving?

When someone is grieving or mourning it's often difficult to know what to do or say to them. This feeling is a common experience, and may arise due to fears we will say something thoughtless, or will cause greater sadness for the bereaved friend when we bring up the loss. Or maybe, in a desire to comfort and support those who are grieving, we want to say or do just the right thing that will help the bereaved feel happy or find healing.

The discomfort arises as well because it's hard to be with someone who is sad, or to see a friend hurting. Loss, and especially death, makes many of us uncomfortable, perhaps due to feelings about our mortality, or sense of how the world should work, or fear of the unknown, or because we feel powerless to make things better when others suffer a loss. Whatever the source of uneasiness, those who befriend and support the bereaved are often at a loss for words.

Each situation regarding loss and grief is unique. What may be fine to say in one instance may be inappropriate in another. However, there are some common guidelines and phrases that are helpful, or that should be avoided, when talking with someone who is grieving. The following lists are not exhaustive regarding what to say or not say, but hopefully will offer examples for comforting the bereaved. Remember that you cannot take away the pain, but you can be a resource of support and even hope and healing.

Possible things to say to a friend, acquaintance, or loved one who is grieving (see also the websites listed at the end of this book):

(1) The first thing to consider is whether you need to say anything at all. Being present with and listening to the person grieving is one of the most important things a friend or family member can do.

(2) Do not be afraid to talk about or mention the person who died, or talk about the pet lost, or refer to the situation that underlies the grief. However, be sensitive to the needs of the bereaved and what they are willing to talk about. For example, a daughter lost her mother, Gloria, in the summer. When the extended family gathered for Thanksgiving dinner, no one mentioned the mother's name. The daughter was heartbroken and felt the other family members' refusal to speak her mother's name aloud dishonored her life and memory. Although the daughter was not looking for a deep conversation about her (and their) loss, simply saying "we miss Gloria" would have acknowledged her mother's death and the feelings that accompanied the loss.

(3) Acknowledge the pain and sadness.

(4) "If you can (or "if you're ready") tell me more about your brother. He was such a special person."

(5) "You can talk to me about your dad any time you want."

(6) "I am so saddened by your loss."

(7) "Feeling sadness and anger is normal," or "Feeling grief is normal."

(8) "Do you want to talk about it?"

(9) "Pets are such a part of the family. I know you will miss Sophie."

(10) "I'm thinking about you/praying for you."
(11) "I remember when your sister. . . ." Sharing a memory that is dear to you can be helpful.
(12) "I miss him too, so I can only imagine the pain you're feeling."
(13) "I wish I had the words to help—just know that I am here for you."
(14) "This really sucks," or "This is really hard."
(15) "I've got a big shoulder, so don't be afraid to let go and feel what you need to feel."
(16) "Whenever you're ready, I am willing to listen and help if I can. . . ." You can help a friend do things like plan for the funeral, think about other job possibilities, brainstorm a new direction in life or college to attend, research ways to participate in charitable organizations that offer a connection to the loved one or friend they lost. Of course, timing is critical regarding how and when to offer help.

Examples of what not to do and say:

(1) Avoid being overly cheery or looking for a bright side.
(2) "You'll be stronger because of this," or "Be brave."
(3) "It's God's plan," or "This is God's will."
(4) "You have other siblings" (or friends, or "at least you have your mother").
(5) "They're in a better place."
(6) "Stop being so dramatic," or dismissing the loss (e.g., the death of a pet, or loss of a relationship)
(7) "It's time to move on," or "Get over it."
(8) "I know how you feel." Even if you have lost someone close, or experienced a similar loss, does not mean you know how the friend or loved one feels. Each individual's grief and path are unique. The bereaved may be open to your comfort and advice because they know about your loss, whatever it may be. However, be careful not to equate the feelings and circumstances and be mindful of the process the friend needs to deal with.
(9) "Please stop crying, it will be alright," or "Get it together."
(10) "Shouldn't you be more upset?" Avoid telling others how to grieve.
(11) "Oh, you'll find another boyfriend/girlfriend."
(12) "At least your grandmother lived to 93."
(13) "You'll get into another school, just keep trying."
(14) "Don't you think it's time to get another pet."
(15) "Time heals all wounds."
(16) Don't try to answer the question "Why?"

33. What can help when you're grieving?

Grief is a natural part of life that embraces a number of possible reactions and paths. Although a common experience, it's not easy to endure and typically involves emotional distress, mental struggle, spiritual challenge, fatigue and a heaviness about life. For the teenager and young adult dealing with loss, on top of other changes and challenges at this moment, life can be demanding and stressful. However, despite the weightiness of bereavement, the process of grief can be a way to explore one's inner depths, find new meaning and move toward healing and a new normal. There are a number of suggestions to keep in mind when faced with a significant loss, ideas that have helped others along the journey.

For teenagers and adults alike, self-care is important to managing life and health. The same is especially true for those dealing with grief. The top recommendation for self-care by the Dougy Center, a national center for grieving children, youth, and young adults, *is to breathe*. Keeping mindful of one's breath—slowing the breath down or taking deep breaths repeatedly when stressed or anxious—is a common meditative practice and beneficial for health. There are other commonsense practices that are helpful too, but often forgotten or overlooked when one is dealing with loss and grief. Maintaining a healthy diet, drinking enough water or fluids, exercising—either a new exercise routine or simply walking or moving your body, getting enough sleep, and paying attention to physical hygiene are all important ways to support physical and mental health. They also happen to be critical for health and stability as one grieves.

When a loved one or friend dies, it can be beneficial to find a creative outlet—like creating art, such as a mural or collage on paper or on the computer. Playing music, or simply listening to music, or creating a play list of favorite songs the deceased would have liked can also be helpful and keep the bereaved connected to the person who died. Getting together with friends to see a movie or play a video game or just hang out are other ways to cope with the strong emotions and loss. At times the bereaved teenager or young adult needs a break from the grief, to become immersed in something happy or fun, not as a way to avoid the pain, but as a way to conserve or generate needed energy and emotional resources for the journey ahead. Celebrating milestones and laughing (e.g., laughing at funny stories about the person who died) are other ways to find solace and relief. Some may find consolation in spiritual practices and rituals. Lighting a candle, prayer, questioning or seeking comfort from God, spending time in nature, or practicing gratitude are a few of the ways that touch a young person's spiritual health and path of grief.

Finding ways to remember, be connected to, or honor a loved one or friend who died is also valuable for young people who are grieving. Traditional rituals like the funeral or memorial service are important for those mourning and grieving, especially when the bereaved teenager or young adult can help with the planning or participate in the service. Creating a memorial, visiting a place that was important to the deceased loved one or friend, going to the gravesite and keeping it up or leaving flowers have been helpful to many generations of the bereaved. Some who have lost loved ones "talk with them" on a hike, or in a special place, or when struggling with a problem. In a number of cultures and families, speaking with the dead may feel strange or uncomfortable, while in others such a connection is normal and commonplace (see Questions 37 and 39). Another way to remember and connect is to find something the person who died owned to hold on to as a keepsake. Memory boxes with pictures or other items, creating a photo or video album on the computer, or sharing stories and memories of the deceased with friends can also help. Sharing pictures and memories through social or digital media is another possibility, which also allows for conversation with others who may share experiences around loss. Staying connected in a healthy way to the deceased is beneficial for the grieving process. However, if the bereaved begins to have constant, daily thoughts about the deceased at the expense of other thoughts and activities, or preoccupied with how their loved one or friend died, then grief can become unhealthy, especially if such obsession interrupts normal functioning.

Journaling is also a relatively easy and valuable creative exercise for those dealing with significant emotions, struggles, meaning and purpose. Journaling does not have to consist of perfect sentence structure or just the right words. It is simply a personal way to sort out feelings, reflect and think about life. One of the most significant books about grief, *A Grief Observed*, was written by C.S. Lewis after the death of his wife. It was compiled from notebooks, or journals, that Lewis kept to sort out his feelings, faith, and life. At the end of the book he writes, "In so far as this record was a defence against total collapse, a safety valve, it has done some good." The point of journaling, and many other suggestions mentioned, is to provide a safety valve, to assist the bereaved in their search for healing, health, new meaning and purpose.

One of the most helpful and crucial ways to find help when grieving is to develop a healthy support network. Although teenagers and young adults often withdraw or find it difficult to share thoughts and feelings with parents or friends they fear will not understand, it's important for bereaved young people to talk with someone they can trust. Oftentimes, such trusted individuals are friends and family, but can be other dependable and empathetic adults, like a teacher, counselor, clergy, or family friend. It can also be helpful for the bereaved, or someone acting on their behalf, to tell teachers at school or employers about the loss so they will be aware and accommodate times when grief may affect work or attendance (see Question 22). There are also many support groups available through hospice or at local organizations that provide bereavement services. Support sites are also available online and include online memorials, internet bereavement support groups, and peer-support webpages where participants can ask questions of other teenagers and young adults facing significant loss. Some of these resources are listed at the end of the book.

Although essential to have others who support, it's also important for teenagers and young adults to create time and space to be alone, as long as alone time is not constant and a way to avoid others or memories of the loss. Spending time alone allows for journaling, creativity, reflection, and space from having to answer questions or deal constantly with the loss. Whether alone, or with others, it is crucial for the bereaved to give themselves permission to feel the feelings they need to feel. If grief goes on too long, if depression deepens, or there are other symptoms that signal unhealthy grief (see especially Questions 5, 27, and 29) it is crucial to seek bereavement counselors (see Question 34), other mental health professionals or hotlines for various forms of crucial need.

34. What are grief/bereavement counselors and how can they help?

When a teenager or young adult faces the death of someone close, it is important to enlist support from trusted family and friends. Other individuals like teachers, clergy or staff at high schools and colleges can also provide critical support in times of loss. There are other organizations and persons who specialize in counseling around grief and loss that can also be enlisted, especially when a young person is struggling.

Grief is a normal process that occurs after a loss, especially the death of someone close. Each person deals with loss in their own way and in their own time depending on numerous factors (see Questions 1 and 21). The first few weeks after a loss can be especially intense and is typically followed by weeks and months where sadness and other usual responses lessen in intensity. In this time, grief may come and go as the person begins to adjust to the loss and finds a way to healing and a new way of life.

However, for some bereaved young people, the road is not so smooth. If someone who suffers loss is dealing with a lot of distress, or if the grief is unrelenting and overwhelming, or intrudes on normal daily routines to a great extent, then it may be time to seek mental health or other professionals to help.

One source of support are *bereavement counselors*. They are trained to help those who have suffered loss to process grief, especially when the bereaved is dealing with considerable stumbling blocks along the way. These counselors provide a safe space to talk about loss and express feelings that may be hard to share with others. They also can suggest different avenues for grief and mourning, help the bereaved to adjust to the loss, or provide ideas for healthy connection to the deceased through memory, ritual, and reflection. In short, bereavement counselors can assist the bereaved with dealing with loss, finding meaning and carrying on with life. These counselors can meet with clients individually, but also lead support groups.

Bereavement counselors come from a variety of backgrounds—mental health and counseling, social work, nursing, family therapy, ministry, and research psychology. A few may have doctoral degrees, but most have master's degrees in appropriate fields as well as other critical training and certification. For example, a number of bereavement specialists are Licensed Professional Counselors (LPC), Licensed Clinical Social Workers (LCSW) or Licensed Marriage and Family Therapists (LFMT). They also gain education and skills through certification as Clinical Trauma Professionals, Advanced Bereavement Facilitators, or in some other counseling specialty related to grief and loss. Most gain knowledge and proficiency through certification in Thanatology, the study of death, dying and the needs associated with loss.

Bereavement counselors are often part of an organization that helps those who are grieving or have suffered loss. These organizations provide counseling services, as well as articles, videos, support groups, and other resources. The website hellogrief.org has a partial list of such organizations listed by state. Bereavement counselors are also part of the care team for hospice organizations. Hospice care is often sought out for those who are suffering from a life-limiting illness. A form of palliative care (see Glossary), hospice care is specifically for those patients that are no longer receiving curative treatment and have been diagnosed with six months or less to live. Hospice provides a number of services for the patient and families, including bereavement care. Hospice organizations that receive Medicare funding (nearly all do), are mandated to provide bereavement services before and after a death. The services are to be coordinated by a qualified counselor with experience, training and education in grief and loss counseling. Bereavement services are required to be offered up to thirteen months after the death of a loved one. Some hospice organizations provide services for longer, usually up to eighteen months. The bereavement counselor that works with a hospice is in contact with the family before and soon after the death, but only offers counsel when asked or invited. They also provide leadership for support groups, some specialized, for family members who lost a loved one.

Although bereavement counselors receive suitable education and training, they are not typically qualified psychologists or psychiatrists, and usually refrain from dealing with serious episodes of complicated grief (see Question 27), major depression (see Question 5), or other acute mental health disorders connected to grief. However, some are especially trained in suicide bereavement or have special training or skills to deal with more difficult issues. In either case, ethical and professional standards require bereavement counselors to refer a bereaved client to a more qualified specialist when necessary. Bereavement counselors may also be known as Grief Counselors, while those who deal with more serious mental health issues and more traumatic grief responses would be considered Grief Therapists.

Young people experiencing normal grief responses are not usually in need of bereavement counselors. Feeling sadness, or mild anxiety, having episodes of crying, experiencing stomach upset, some loss of sleep, or other responses (see Questions 1 and 5), especially in the first few weeks, are part of a characteristic pattern of grief. Some of these responses may come and go over a longer period as well. However, if grief reactions and symptoms become more acute and prolonged, and begin to interfere with daily functioning, then bereavement care or other mental health professionals could be needed and helpful. Whatever the reactions may be, seeing a bereavement specialist for assessment, or being included in a support group for teens and/or young adults could be helpful to process and adapt to the loss.

35. Who else can help when I'm grieving?

An important aspect of healthy grieving involves finding support from friends, trusted adults, support groups or others. Although it may be difficult for the bereaved young person to reach out, especially when emotions are raw and challenging to deal with, being able to talk about feelings, fears, memories, and concerns is an essential aspect of healing and adapting to the loss. Friends are a natural support group. Although they may not completely understand the depth of the grieving person's loss or be able to fully empathize with the feelings being experienced, close friends can be an encouragement or simply be there to listen. Not every friend will be comfortable dealing with death, but some are capable of focusing attention on the needs of the bereaved. Such friends may also know the person who died and can be more keenly aware of the loss. Peers can also engage the grieving friend in familiar activities and routines, which can help lessen the intense feelings of loss.

Parents and other trusted family members are important for support of the grieving teenager or young adult as well. Of course, parents may struggle with their own loss if the deceased is a son or daughter, family member or close acquaintance of the family. Or, parents may have problems understanding the depth of a young person's particular loss. However, if they are able to provide support, parental involvement is crucial for the grieving teenager or young adult. Loss can have a destabilizing effect on the bereaved, and a parent's healthy reaction to the death, whether of a family or friend, can provide needed stability. Although a teen may be developing their own identity apart from the parents and family, family members still know the young person in ways different from others. Such familiarity and knowledge can be a great asset for helping the grieving teen or young adult. Also, the parent may be able to share or discuss important information about the circumstances around the death in ways that are helpful and reassuring.

Other family members can be helpful as well, especially if there is a strong bond between the grieving young person and a trusted relative. A favorite aunt may be able to provide unique care, or a sibling close in age could also be a great support. The ability to offer needed help will certainly depend on the depth of the relationship with the grieving teen or young adult. Care is often enhanced if the relative lives close by, or is able to provide consistent communication.

There are other trusted adults who may be able to provide support for the bereaved. A favorite teacher at school could be someone that will listen and provide wisdom, especially if the death involved a classmate. Teachers can also offer suggestions and help for the student as they negotiate classes, tests, and studies. School counselors are also trained to help in crisis situations. Counselors may also be aware of resources that parents or other adults may be unacquainted with, and can facilitate particular needs the student may have regarding schoolwork or contacting teachers. Ministers or clergy are another source of aid and comfort. They are trained to help in times of crisis, especially when there is a death of a loved one or friend. If faith is important (see Question 37) consulting a minister may be helpful since a significant loss can challenge long-held feelings and beliefs. Clergy can also bring families or groups together for needed conversation and are skilled at planning funerals or memorials. Teachers, counselors, and clergy are all required to ensure confidentiality.

There are other groups that can be helpful too, like a Student Services department or the Dean's office at a college or university (see Question 22). Larger school districts may have similar resources for high school students, though the particular school and staff may be the most helpful means for assistance. Support groups are also available through counselors, religious organizations or other groups, and associations dedicated to helping those who have suffered loss. For example, hellogreif.org has a state by state list of organizations that provide help and many include support groups. Hospice organizations (see Question 34) typically offer bereavement care for eighteen months after the death of a loved one or friend, and some offer support groups specifically for teenagers and young adults. Organizations that deal with concerns around grieving a death may also provide bereavement counselors (see Question 34), support groups, written and video resources (see Directory of Resources for selected organizations).

There are a number of people who can help when a young person is grieving, but not every adult or friend is capable of assisting. Certain attitudes and qualities are beneficial when aiding and caring for the bereaved. The ability to listen well and be a nonanxious presence are vital skills for those who journey with individuals who have suffered loss, as are empathy and being nonjudgmental. Understanding and reflecting back feelings expressed by the grieving young person without appraisal or criticism is extremely important. Those who provide support for the bereaved teenager or young adult also exhibit compassion, honesty, warmth, and caring. Typically, one who has suffered loss, no matter their age, turn to those they trust and respect, or who possess the knowledge and resources that can aid the grieving person. Sometimes, the trusted confidant is dealing with the same loss and is able to model healthy grief. Finally, self-awareness and being vulnerable are also important traits for the one who offers care and are usually attributes gained through experience and maturity. Self-aware individuals have reflected on life experience and feelings, and typically have a deeper understanding and comfort level talking about things like death, meaning, life, and purpose. Being vulnerable allows someone to be open to another's pain, even when it touches on the painful aspects of their life. Being vulnerable is not about helplessness or exploiting weakness. Rather, healthy vulnerability is about making deep connections with others and requires a strong sense of limits, self-understanding, insight, and care.

Getting needed support, whatever the source, is crucial. Grief can be destabilizing and cause struggle in simple daily routines and life circumstances. Identity, beliefs, and world view may also be challenged. Therefore, having a trusted person to talk to, or a support group that understands can aid the grieving process. It's also very helpful, especially at school, to have adult staff who are aware of the circumstances regarding a young person's loss. Such advocates can help in a discreet and confidential way to deal with the various needs of the grieving student.

36. What is resilience and how does it affect bereavement and grief?

Although the journey of grief is unique to each person, it usually takes on familiar patterns and involves reactions that are common. Some believe grief always involves a particular set of reactions and feelings that endure for a period of time. Others feel the process of grief requires the completion of particular tasks or stages, or will need the assistance of trained professionals, support groups or therapy. If tasks or stages are not completed, or if someone seems to recover too quickly, there are some theorists who believe the bereaved is in denial or will suffer delayed grief. However, current studies show a more varied picture and suggest the phenomenon of delayed grief is not empirically verifiable.

For some who have suffered loss, deep struggles do occur. Contemporary research indicates 10-20 percent of bereaved persons experience complicated or prolonged grief (see Question 27) and typically need to engage the services of a mental health or bereavement specialist. Another sizeable group experiences acute grief and recovers more slowly, though they find healing in a gradual way over a few months to a year, or even two. However, recent studies have shown that most bereaved persons, or those suffering traumatic events (45–60%), find a way to adjust and carry on with their lives relatively quickly. Even though they may experience shock, anger, and other usual grief reactions, or occasional feelings of sadness from time to time, they adapt and return to normal, everyday life with the ability to function, find meaning, and live healthy lives. A number of scholars indicate that such persons exhibit *resilience*. These researchers suggest that excessive attention is given to the study of grief and bereavement that lasts over longer periods of time, or that leads to complicated grief. They believe such intense focus ignores needed exploration around the significant number of those who face loss, yet find ways to adapt on their own. Recent evidence about resilience challenge long-held beliefs about various aspects of the grief process, including denial, delayed grief, and the role of positive emotions.

Although resilience research or resilience science is a relatively new field, it crosses a number of disciplines including psychology, education, child development, and bereavement. More recent longitudinal studies (studies of persons over a period of time) of those who have faced loss, as well as exploration of persons experiencing early childhood trauma or trauma in adulthood, have found that many tend to adapt, adjust, find meaning, and carry on with life. The findings do not suggest judgment regarding those who are resilient versus those who are not, but simply counter a perceived myth that all bereaved persons must struggle with loss and grief with particular reactions in traditionally accepted ways.

Like grief, resilience can be defined in a variety of ways. For purposes here, resilience will be defined as the capacity to cope with or adapt to a loss in healthy ways. The definition includes finding stability and returning to healthy functioning as well as the ability to learn from the loss or finding new meaning. Resilience also implies timing that is relatively quick (e.g., within weeks or a few months).

Although most of the studies around resilience involves adults, similar findings have been found when studying those who suffered trauma or traumatic events in childhood. However, in light of the varied and complex developmental tasks and events in the life of a teenager and young adult, it may be difficult to assume that resilience occurs at the same rate as that found in studies involving adults or children (see Question 6). Even so, some young people find a way back to normal, everyday life after a significant loss without missing a beat, while others may struggle for longer periods of time. Other young adults or teenagers may develop symptoms of complicated grief or some type of anxiety disorder. Again, mentioning the different types and levels of reactions are not indicated as a way to judge, but to be aware of the many and varied ways grief can occur.

Since young people experience the same variety of grief responses as adults do, including resilience, considering what research tells us about characteristics that foster resilience can be informative and helpful. Since the research is somewhat new, there is no universally accepted list or official designation regarding the emotional, psychological, and relational qualities characteristic for resilience or resilient people. However, there are patterns and attributes that are emerging. Typically, resilient people have a support group of friends and family, or a young person may have a trusted adult they can talk to or depend on. The relationship with the lost loved one is also critical. Usually, resilient people find comfort in the memories they have of the person who died. Positive memories are easier when the relationship was solid, healthy, supportive, and/or loving. Some resilient people may continue strong memories by continuing a favorite activity they shared with the person lost, like attending sports events, or by volunteering for a group or cause important to the deceased. If a person already has adaptive skills when faced with adversity, then such abilities can help. Confidence, optimism, and better health, unsurprisingly, also encourage a resilient outlook. Other positive life circumstances, like the family's financial status, or greater choices regarding education or future possibilities can also aid resilience. The ability to laugh and experience other appropriate positive emotions, even when adversity strikes, can be influential. Although scientific evidence is not conclusive, genetics may have some influence on a person's capacity to be resilient.

There are also events, circumstances, and behaviors that can hinder resilience, or a relatively quick return to normal function and adapting well after a loss. When a bereaved person misuses avoidance and distraction as coping mechanisms, this can get in the way of embracing positive memories, engaging in helpful conversations with others or dealing with emotional aspects of the loss. Multiple childhood traumas can also affect a teenager's ability to find constructive ways to deal with the loss. The presence of other major stresses in life can also be a hindrance, as well as experiencing multiple losses in a short period of time or at once. If the bereaved witnesses the violent death of a friend or loved one, or has some other trauma associated with the death (like with suicide), then the young person will likely have struggles with grief. A poor family environment, unresolved issues between the young person and the person who died, a dysfunctional or abusive relationship with the deceased, or a history of anxiety disorders can also lead to a longer grief process or lead to complicated grief.

Young people who experience none of these difficulties can still encounter longer periods of bereavement and struggle, or even deal with complicated grief. On the other hand, persons who have challenges in life can still find their way to health and healing fairly quickly with helpful support. The path of grief is unique for each person and one can never predict what may happen when the right person consoles, the bereaved finds unexpected inner resources, or if some other challenge will appear, or family and friends act in bewildering ways. Any teenager or young adult facing the pain of loss should be supported and allowed to experience the grief journey in the way needed. In these moments, each young person needs appropriate care and encouragement as they find their way to heal-ing and new meaning.

In certain cultures, like the United States, death is often difficult to speak about and is surrounded by fear and misunderstanding. So, when death happens or someone is affected by the loss of someone close, there is a tendency to avoid conversation or expect the bereaved to move on from sadness or other challenging feelings. Often, societal or peer pressure leads those suffering losses to ignore their emotional and psychological pain, or feel that something is wrong with them if they do not get back to normal. Careless focus on resilience as the ideal way for persons to grieve, or as the definition of healthy grief can feed into such cultural avoidance and lead to unhealthy responses and practices around bereavement. Teenage and young adult years are often tumultuous or challenging because so many changes are happening physically, emotionally, socially, and psychologi-cally. These challenges will affect the way one grieves. So, it's important to stress that resilience is just one of the many ways that healthy grief can happen. Even though many recover quickly, the way one handles some-thing as complex and varied as grief is not an indicator of what is normal or natural or conventional. How one deals with grief is not a judgment on their abilities or value as a person. Grief needs to take the path necessary for the individual, and it is good to keep in mind the power of grief and the potential it has for nourishing life-giving change no matter the path it may take.

37. How can my spirituality or religious community affect the grieving process?

Spirituality, faith, and belief are an important part of how some young people make meaning in their lives, or are a part of their family's values and practices. Some define spirituality as being explicitly oriented toward God or a higher power, while others address spirituality in broader terms around meaning and lived experience with no mention of a divine being or the sacred. Simply put, spirituality encompasses a person's search for meaning and purpose and the way they express the search, their values and beliefs, and the way they find connection to the self, others, the sig-nificant or the sacred. The significant for some could be family, an orga-nization or social cause, while the sacred might encompass nature, the divine or some overarching moral principle that sustains life.

Teenagers and those approaching adulthood often identify with the spirituality and religious beliefs of their family in some fashion, from strict adherence to a family's spiritual tradition to outright rejection. Young people are also at a time of life where many changes are happening around things like meaning and purpose and establishing a self-identity separate from their family. Even in the midst of changes, though, some teenagers or young adults might continue to hold to the conventional beliefs of their upbringing, while others begin considering alternative ways of perceiving the spiritual side of themselves. In a time of loss, one's view of the world can be altered and changed, which may include the possibility of modifying or completely changing religious or spiritual values. What may have provided comfort and safety in the past is often challenged in the midst of a significant loss. God's protection or existence might be questioned, or a friend's violent death might cause a young person to question if there is good in the world. Or, someone who never believed in, or thought about anything beyond immediate existence might begin to wish for, or believe in some type of afterlife. Still others will find comfort in their spirituality and beliefs, gaining a sense of peace because of God's presence or their conviction that all things will come to a good end, or believing that life *and* death are part of a larger spirit or purpose.

There are a number of ways a young person's spirituality can be of help when dealing with grief and loss. Typical spiritual practices like prayer and journaling can offer needed outlets for sadness and anger, provide a chance to seek inner resources of faith and strength, or seek the comfort of God or a higher power. Meditation can help quiet the mind and allow space for healing and greater attentiveness to the sacred. Walks in nature or yoga practice can touch the soul in ways that give a depth of perspective, a chance to seek clarity, or may simply be a way to practice self-care. Deep breathing can be an essential part of healing too, as can singing, reading scripture or poetry, finding avenues to help others, or spending time with those who share in a particular faith or spiritual expression

Several important questions around faith and spirituality involve whether one's spiritual convictions facilitate or impede grief, and if their beliefs focus on judgment or hope. For instance, if a person's belief system involves divine judgment or punishment, then the grief process can be saddled with concerns about the soul of their dead loved one, leading to worries which could hinder a sense of acceptance, healing, or moving on. A faith practice that involves a higher power that is compassionate and loving may help the bereaved feel assurance about the destiny of their loved one. Such feelings may also allow for a sense of hope and finding new meaning. Some spiritual practices may lead to deeper meaning and greater perspective, but can also be used to avoid the difficult emotions and questions.

It's essential that teenagers and young adults be able to ask questions and express doubts about faith, feel anger at God or the universe, or deal with other thoughts and feelings in an honest and candid way. It is helpful to have adults willing to be a nonjudgmental presence, giving a chance for the bereaved young person to explore their feelings and beliefs. For some, a spiritual home is a needed source of comfort and peace, a safe place to bring the struggles and doubt that often accompany grief. For others, their faith tradition may be constricting, or overly harsh, and may lead to questioning one's world view or family traditions in ways that may be isolating. In either case, young people (and many others) want to know they are not alone in their questions, and that their spiritual selves will not be lost in the midst of grief and mourning.

Religious communities, or groups that share transcendent values, can be a help and offer support, though some may be more conducive to providing a sense of peace, or encouraging and supporting healthy grief. Even traditions that are more judgmental can be a safe place for some, especially if they need absolute certainty about their own life and choices, or assurance about life and the divine working in a certain way. However, for many, openness, mercy, forgiveness, and benevolence are more important as they explore their spirituality in the face of death and significant loss.

Religious communities can also be of help around practical aspects of death and dying and usually have rituals that offer comfort and meaning. Typically, funeral or memorial services that focus on remembrance, celebration of life, giving the deceased over to God or another power or spirit, is an essential part of a young person's grief process. If the person who died was an immediate family member or close friend, it is helpful for the teenager or young adult to be given a chance to participate in some ways in the funeral service.

Many faith traditions speak a particular language that can be beneficial as a young person sorts out their grief. For example, helpful concepts and values like gratitude, forgiveness, divine presence, the end of suffering, achieving a higher state of consciousness, becoming part of something larger than ourselves, receiving benevolent care, and hope are all part of the focus of many spiritual and religious traditions. On the other hand, some traditions focus on exclusion, judgment, and eternal punishment, which may get in the way of healthy grief for the bereaved.

Different religious traditions and spiritualties offer particular beliefs a young person may embrace about the possibility of continued existence for the deceased, or a trust that death is not the end (see also Question 38). Many are comforted by the conviction they will see their loved ones again, or that they can remain connected in some spiritual way.

Those who are certain there is nothing beyond our existence now may have trouble letting go or become deeply sad about what was or will be missed when someone close dies. On the other hand, such a belief can help a young person be grateful for the time shared with their friend or loved one.

Oftentimes, a teenager or young adult and their family can find solace and comfort through the care of a faith community. In many cases, those who are part of a temple, church, synagogue, or some other spiritually oriented organization (like Alcoholics Anonymous), will rally around those who are bereaved and dealing with grief. Members of the group may offer meals, rides or be willing to talk and offer emotional support. Many spiritual leaders can also be relied on to offer a safe place for questions, anger, sadness or other feelings that accompany bereavement. However, a young person may shy away from a religious tradition because it resists the necessity for grief, or because they feel unsafe expressing doubts or questions about faith, or if they feel judged for being angry at God.

The grief journey can be a challenge for young people and will certainly test their spirituality and beliefs. Even so, the teenager or young adult's spirituality and religious tradition has the potential for being a source of support, comfort and exploration in this journey. Hopefully, a bereaved teenager's tradition or spiritual beliefs will give attention to their deepest questions and needs, and provide room to explore and uncover aspects of life that give meaning and purpose in the face of loss.

❖❖❖

Other Important Questions

38. What happens after I die?

An interest in the afterlife reaches far into human history and ancient civilizations and is even prevalent today. The concepts and beliefs surrounding life after death have been diverse and numerous, even within particular religious traditions. It is not possible in the scope of this book to address the multitude beliefs and understandings that may answer the question "what happens after I die?" However, a brief sketch of certain viewpoints will be provided to focus attention on how a belief or understanding in the afterlife might affect bereavement.

One of the critical needs for some who believe in a life after death is the desire to maintain a connection to the person who died. Maintaining healthy connections, through memory or other means, has often had a positive effect on the ability of bereaved persons to cope, find new meaning, and heal. So, believing a loved one or friend who dies can still exist in an afterlife allows for hope that some type of interaction or communication with them is possible. Some bereaved young people and adults feel there is a thin veil between this word and the next, allowing loved ones who have died to watch over their family and friends, or simply allow some sense of continued relationship and presence. There are many a story of such connection and contact in literature, research studies, and personal accounts.

While traditions or faith experience about the afterlife provides a source of comfort to some grieving loss, the death of a friend or loved one may lead to anxiety or fear regarding their eternal resting place, especially if the faith tradition includes eternal judgment and punishment. Such beliefs may have negative effects on bereavement and healing (see Question 37). It's also the case that the death of someone close may challenge long-held beliefs and thoughts of the bereaved regarding what happens after we die, or about life itself. Such reflection may especially be true among teenagers and young adults engaged in a critical stage of forming values, beliefs, and life principles (see Question 6).

There are numerous ways that people think about the afterlife. One of the most well-known and common expressions of life after death in literature, philosophy, religious texts, media, and other sources (especially in the west) is some concept or representation of heaven and hell. The monotheistic religions—Judaism, Christianity, and Islam—include some representation of heaven or hell as possible eternal resting places. Other faith traditions, like Buddhism and Hinduism, also convey a belief in a heaven or hell, though these may not symbolize the final resting place for those who die.

According to data from a 2014 study by the Pew Research Center, 72 percent of the U.S. population believes in heaven and 58 percent believes in hell. Persons of Christian and Muslim faith traditions had the highest percentage scores while atheists, unsurprisingly, had the lowest (though 5% of atheists believed in heaven and 3% believed in hell). For other countries, especially those in certain parts of Europe and Asia, the percentages are much lower regarding a belief in heaven and hell, while in some countries in Europe, Southeast Asia, and the Americas, the percentages are comparable or higher than the United States.

Such beliefs can influence the process of grief for the bereaved, whether adults, teenagers, or children. For some, it is a comfort to know their loved one is in heaven. There are various beliefs about a heavenly realm where loved ones are cared for by a supreme being or continue to live in a way beyond the limitations of earthly existence. Heaven is often thought of as a place of peace, where there is no suffering, trials or tribulations, and where one lives in bliss with a deeper connection to God and others. There are many stories about those comforted by a belief in heaven, who insist death is not a final goodbye, and are assured they will see their friend or loved one again. For example, a family may share grief about the loss of a fifteen-year-old daughter and sister, but are able to have hope because they believe they will see her again. A youth relates that she began to think about heaven after her best friend died—and wonders what reuniting with her friend might be like. Those who have such beliefs may find it easier to cope and find healing.

Of course, the idea of heaven may be a source of struggle for some. Even if a bereaved person believes they will see their loved ones again, there is still a temporary separation, which will be less of a comfort and cause more anguish as time goes by. Typically, people who believe in heaven are also convinced there is a hell, which for some is a place of punishment and torment. Since heaven is not a sure thing, depending on the way heaven and hell are conceived, some bereaved teenagers and young adults may encounter greater distress and fear about what happens after a loved one or friend dies. Instead of being comforted by the thought of eternal union with family, friends, and a higher being, they may worry about being separated for eternity from those they love. Beliefs about heaven or hell are far from uniform. There are those who believe in a literal place, while others believe it is a state of mind or consciousness. Some believe heaven is one place, while others understand heaven to consist of stages or several realms. Certain religious traditions feel that the afterlife, even in heaven, consists of a continued striving toward some ultimate goal or attainment. Each of these beliefs can be a comfort or a challenge when a loved one dies.

There are, of course, many other beliefs about what happens after a person dies. For instance, another widespread view about the afterlife is expressed in Hinduism and Buddhism. In very simple terms, these faith traditions maintain that existence consists of a cycle of life, death and rebirth, which is also a cycle of suffering. However, movement through the series of births, deaths and rebirths is essential for escaping the cycle of suffering and reaching or attaining nirvana, or paradise. Those who believe in this way consider death a natural and welcome part of life, since through death an essential part of the deceased's consciousness continues on in life anew through reincarnation. Though this may be a comfort, ancient texts and beliefs about reincarnation do not speak of, or guarantee, a reuniting with loved ones or friends. In traditional Hindu and Buddhist thought, there is no idea of an individual person with a memory of a previous life, returning to earth, or moving on to some heavenly realm for eternity. There is also an understanding that at death we shed the personal, and that our true or essential self is understood best as being grounded in a universal, ageless soul which negates a personal existence. Such beliefs can offer opportunities for comfort to the bereaved, but can also lead to deep sadness that the personhood of their friend or loved one no longer exists.

For some teenagers and young adults there may be uncertainty or loosely held beliefs regarding the afterlife. These notions may include some belief that our soul or essence returns to some all-encompassing energy or spirit. Others may have a vague sense that the arc of the universe or grand purpose of God or a supreme being is to bring an ultimate healing and wholeness to existence. For other young people, a belief in the afterlife does not square with their experience or conflicts with a more scientific view. Since we often want to justify our beliefs, to have some sense of proof or scientific validity, thoughts about what happens after we die are unhelpful or matter little to bereavement and feelings about life and death. Still others agree with the well-known quote from Ernst Becker in his book *The Denial of Death*: "What does it mean to be a self-conscious animal? The idea is ludicrous, if it is not monstrous. It means to know that one is food for worms." Of course, any belief that there is nothing beyond our earthly existence can offer little comfort to the grieving, unless the focus of the bereaved is on the good life the deceased lived or memories of the relationship the bereaved enjoyed with them. However, when trying to make sense of a sudden death, or the loss of a close friend, the absence of some hope for continued existence may hinder the ability to grieve well, find new meaning and heal.

There are many other viewpoints concerning the afterlife, some deeply metaphysical and esoteric, while others may be more simplistic. What does seem to be of concern to many who grieve is a sense that there is something beyond this life and that in some way we can remain connected to loved ones and friends that have died. Some are also concerned about where their loved one has gone, what eternity may be like, and whether a reuniting of some kind will take place. In many cases the grieving teenager and young adult may simply be seeking to grasp hold of an idea or belief that will offer a sense of hope and continued existence.

The focus in the west is often on how we think about the afterlife while other cultures simply live with it and have rituals that enable the bereaved to experience contact and connection with the deceased. For example, "the Day of the Dead" (*El Dia de los Muertos*) is a holiday and tradition celebrated in Mexico and in other parts of the world. In this custom, death is not feared and is seen as a natural part of human life and existence. The celebration around loved ones who have died includes the practice of erecting an altar to commemorate the life of deceased loved ones. The ritual is done to remember, to encourage visits from the souls of those who have died, and may be connected to the continued spiritual journey of the deceased. The tradition can be traced to ancient traditions and communities from nearly 3,000 years ago. These beliefs mixed with Christian/Catholic practices and now coincide with All Hallows Eve, All Saints Day, and All Souls Day (October 31, November 1, and

November 2). There are other such celebrations around the world that are festive rather than somber (see Question 39).

Although there isn't a consensus about what happens after we die, a belief in the afterlife of some kind often helps the bereaved to cope and heal. In some traditions, death is seen as a natural and welcome part of life, with the anticipation of moments of continued contact and significant, life inspiring memories.

39. How do grief and mourning vary from culture to culture?

The way a young person grieves has to do with a variety of factors including personality, coping skills, family dynamics, the way the parents handle grief, the type and manner of death or loss, and other influences. Culture also influences the way a person grieves and is a powerful facet of a person's life, though most do not recognize its power. Cultural values, rituals, and narratives help shape a young person's beliefs, principles, and behaviors. Though a teenager or young adult may change their sense of how the world works or the beliefs and values they will adopt and accept, one's culture will influence their initial world view and the way their life path unfolds.

Simply put, culture has to do with behaviors and norms of a particular group, society, clan, or civilization. These behaviors and norms include rituals, customs, how knowledge is acquired and operates, history, beliefs, habits, art, values, and a host of other features that give some definition and meaning to the particular group. A young person develops within a particular culture or cultures, and this in turn influences the way a person may grieve and mourn. Although a teenager or young adult can, in time, come to grieve and mourn in ways different from the culture of their youth, initial grief reactions will most likely reflect the values and beliefs of their family, ethnic group, or society.

An exploration of the wide array of differences between and within cultures regarding bereavement is beyond the scope of this book. Even so, it's helpful to offer a few examples of differences regarding attitudes and approaches to death and grief to illustrate cultural variations in specific and general ways. In China there was little to no scholarly study of bereavement until recently (the last twenty years) and the Chinese word used for grief does not capture the nuances and reactions signified by the use of the term in the United States. However, there have been particular burial rituals and other customs around death throughout the

4,000-year history of China, and ancient rituals around the veneration of the dead continue to this day. Practices around death and grief have also been influenced by Taoist, Confucian, and Buddhist ideas and values. Although such rituals have seen changes through history, they continue to shape and inform how people deal with grief and mourning in China. In the United States, much of the literature, blogs, research, and writing about grief and loss focus on the individual's response to grief (though not exclusively). In China, the focus is on family, remembering/venerating the loved one who died, and staying connected to the deceased through ritualistic practices. This focus is expressed in pubic and social ritual. Though personal grief and anguish is common, it's expression is to be private and born in silence.

Though more and more funerals and memorial services in the United States have become celebrations of the life of the deceased and a reminder of a future reconnection with the friend or loved one, North American culture and mindset is still limited by societal avoidance and fear of death. For many, death is the ultimate end, a finality, and the *negation* of life. For others, it may be a gateway to an afterlife, though the afterlife may be something positive and wonderful for some and a misery for others (see Question 38). Whatever the belief may be, typical feelings in many areas of the United States regarding connection between the bereaved and the deceased is simply hoped for in the future, transient, or simply thought unreasonable and nonexistent.

Like China, many other cultures focus in one way or another on community and continued connection. Death is not the end or a negation but is in some way a continuation of life or part of the life cycle (see Question 38). There is less fear of death and more an embrace of the person who died and keeping a connection. Further, in cultures indigenous to Mexico, parts of Africa, and Native American/First Nations tribes and clans, there is a sense that rituals and practices by family and friends help the deceased in some way in the existence they now enjoy. The Mexican celebration *El Dia de la Muertos*, or the "Day of the Dead," is a perfect example (see Question 38). In China the burning of joss paper in honor of deceased loved ones is another. In this ritual, the joss paper is made to look like money or other items important to the deceased that might help or enrich their existence in the afterlife. There are rituals in parts of Africa that are jovial, humorous, and celebratory, and reflect a belief that death is a part of life. In *The Other Side of Sadness*, George Bonanno tells of the Dahomey people of Western Africa who tell off color jokes and tales about the deceased during the funeral. One of the reasons for this practice is for the amusement of the one who died, which assumes a connection with the deceased in ways unfamiliar to many in the United States. In some cultures, ancient rituals and beliefs mingle with adopted religious customs and understandings as well. For instance, though "day of the dead" celebrations have a long history predating Roman Catholic influx into Mexico, modern observance often mixes Catholic religious practice and traditional ritual and meaning.

There are also cultural differences that depend more directly on religious beliefs, rituals, and customs. For example, Jewish custom and belief describes specific and prescribed ritual around bereavement no matter where the Jewish person may live or what other cultural contexts exist. The various rituals include specific blessings and stringent time obligations regarding when the deceased is to be buried as well as mourning rituals (like sitting *shiva*). Particular behaviors are also encouraged or discouraged around the death of a loved one. There are days of remembrance through the year for those who have died, including ritual around the anniversary of a loved one's death. However, Jewish practice focuses on remembering and commemoration, and lacks the sense of connection to the deceased or the celebratory nature of rituals of other cultures. This lack of jovial celebration is understandable since a number of observances focus on victims of the Holocaust and other devastating events in Jewish history. Jewish belief also includes a variety of understandings about the afterlife, from the view there is nothing after this life, to a belief in the reunification of body and soul that will live eternally in some state of bliss or damnation, to many other ideas in-between. These ideas are secondary, though, to an emphasis in Judaism on how a person lives their life on earth.

Christians in the United States and around the world have a variety of beliefs and customs regarding bereavement, death, and the afterlife (see Question 38), though there are basic practices that are fairly uniform. For example, members of different denominations and groups will follow similar ritualistic practices after a death (e.g., there will be a funeral or memorial service and a relatively quick burial of the body or ashes), and many western Christians believe there is little or no connection possible with the deceased until the afterlife. However, there are differences in how the deceased loved one or friend is remembered, variations of belief regarding the afterlife, divergence in the way a funeral happens and whether it is a celebration or subdued occasion, differences regarding whether death is a part of life or an enemy of life, and variance in how one copes with grief and mourning. For example, some conservative or

fundamentalist Protestant groups believe there is little or no need for a
therapist or bereavement counselor. If a person is struggling with grief,
it is due to a lack of faith in God, or a failure to turn to Jesus, or because
a person is wavering in belief. However, there are many Protestants and
other Christians who understand the variety of ways someone can experience grief and the complexity of the human spirit and psyche. Such persons believe the empathetic and caring response to the bereaved person
includes help by secular professionals, support groups and others who may
understand the depth of pain, anxiety and depression. Such help is seen
within the context of a faith that prizes community and a sense that God
inspires those who offer support and comfort.

Within the United States there are also differences in the way various
ethnic cultures may approach death and grief. These differences can be
influenced by countries of origin (e.g., Ghana, China, India, England),
the values and beliefs of individuals and families, as well as the influence
of North American history and culture. For example, racism in the United
States both historically and currently has led many people of color to distrust particular institutions, especially medical institutions, or those that
may deal with death and dying. Since black history in the United States is
filled with brutality, harm, inequality, and other injustices, it would make
sense that grief and mourning might be centered around release, an afterlife filled with peace and justice, cheering, celebrating, and a focus on
altering life circumstances in this world. However, to assume these values
and beliefs for all black persons would be a mistake and lack sensitivity to
those who are suffering loss.

Although Latino/Latina, Native/First Nations, and African American and black cultures are often viewed by some as homogeneous ethnic
groups comprised of individuals with relatively identical cultural values
and rituals, there are actually a wide variety of cultures and values repre-
sented in each ethnic group or tribe. For instance, with regard to death,
grief, and mourning, black Americans may adhere to rituals, values, and
beliefs related to the "Black Church (which is also *hetero*geneous)," Islam,
culturally significant practices from countries of family origin, or other
religious and secular sources. There is no single Native/First Nations culture, and various tribes have a variety of beliefs and rituals around death
and grief. Some Native persons mix traditional rituals and beliefs with
other religious traditions as well. Similarly, Latinx perspectives will be different and may be influenced by indigenous cultural beliefs and practices
within a particular Latin country or area (e.g., Guatemala's population
consists of approximately 23 indigenous groups), or by other religious and
cultural influences.

These are a few examples of various cultural understandings around death, grief, and mourning. They have illustrated some of the differences that exist from culture to culture, such as whether death is a negation of life or a part of the life cycle, beliefs around the afterlife, the nature of the funeral or other rituals around death, connection with the deceased, communal and family bonds and responsibilities regarding the deceased, as well as how emotions are displayed in public. These examples highlight the need for cultural sensitivity when dealing with grief or seeking to help a bereaved friend or loved one.

40. Are media portrayals of death and grief accurate, and can they help me sort out healthy ways to grieve? Can social media help?

The manner in which society has dealt with grief and mourning in the past century has taken on a fairly dramatic change. At one time in U.S. history, the death of loved ones was typically experienced in the home. As the experience of death of loved ones moved from homes to nursing homes, hospitals and other medical institutions, there was a corresponding emotional and psychological effect on the way people reacted to loss and how they processed grief. Over the years, death became less easy to talk about and was often seen as a taboo subject, except at funerals or other similar moments. As personal encounters with death and dying decreased, exposure to death through mass media increased. In a way, media in its many forms became the place where death and dying and related issues could be shown and considered.

Unfortunately, death has been sensationalized and overdone in many instances in video media, as the number of visible deaths on television increased by more than 100 percent since the 1980s. In too many occurrences, little attention was given to the emotional, psychological, and spiritual effects of death, and almost no treatment of issues associated with bereavement. Although there were a number of articles and other treatment of grief and mourning in the United States in the early part of the twentieth century (see Questions 2 and 3), it was not until the second half of the century that attention picked up, especially with the work of Elizabeth Kübler-Ross, the introduction of hospice movement in the United States in the early 1970s, and in some fiction and nonfictional works. By the turn of the twenty-first century more serious attention to loss and grief had been given in most media forms, including video and digital media.

Video and Digital Media

One of the positive features of digital, video, and written media is its ability to draw us into the complex and sometimes messy emotional aspects of the human experience. If done well, such media can paint a fairly reliable picture of environment and circumstances of characters that will feel true to life. A film or show can also depict grief and mourning in ways that mirror the possible feelings and reactions typically experienced by bereaved young people and adults.

Video media has certainly improved over the last two decades in the way grief and mourning are portrayed. Whatsyourgrief.com (see Directory of Resources) lists over seventy movies that treat grief and loss with varying degrees of sensitivity, and some of the best movies and shows can be easily searched online. However, there films and television programs that depict death and loss that have negligible or inadequate treatment of grief, and some still sensationalize death. Crime shows and action movies often pass over any helpful treatment of bereavement, though there are a few exceptions like the crime dramas *River* (BBC1) and *Unforgotten* (ITV).

There are a few other challenges with video media, even for shows that handle grief and loss well. One is the suspension of "real time" in shows and movies, in which the grief and loss depicted does not adequately match the timing of real life. Movies and shows can portray a good model for emotions, thoughts and behaviors that accompany bereavement, but they cannot give an accurate feel for the timing of grief. Also, there is a danger that movies or shows depict the process of grief in ways that sentimentalize death and bereavement in ways not true to life, are overly dramatic, or that fail to acknowledge some of the dark aspects of grief and mourning. Another issue concerns worries about the frequency of the portrayal of death in media, especially in increasingly violent and spectacular ways, and typically without any treatment of grief and loss. Some believe the collective affect may be a numbing of society to death in real life and the pain and reactions that follow. However, many have experienced this concern to be unwarranted.

Despite these challenges, the numerous movies, shows, books, and other media that handle grief well have increased in recent times, and many of them can be instructive and helpful to explore bereavement. In fact, there are courses in college and graduate school on death and dying that use numerous movies, clips from shows and podcasts to open conversation and deepen learning about grief and loss. Of course, taking a class is not required for understanding the lessons and nuances of bereavement that can be gleaned from these productions. However, it is important and helpful for bereaved teenagers and young adults to reflect on and discuss the meaning, challenges, behaviors, and reactions depicted in a movie or show, as well as the ways the media production speaks to the bereaved young person's deepest thoughts and feelings. Conversation with friends and trusted adults is a good way to process, as is connecting with those who have experience with grief or the typical reactions that can arise. At the least, video media can help a bereaved young person get in touch with thoughts and emotions they may be afraid to address, or can help to normalize feelings that seem overwhelming and scary.

Although the scope of this book does not allow for listing the abundance of movies and shows that deal well with grief and loss, a few examples may be helpful to illustrate how a movie or show address classic themes around bereavement. In the well-known *Harry Potter* series created by J. K. Rowling, grief is treated with sensitivity, awareness, and obvious experience by the author. For example, current grief theory points out that continued connection or relationship with the deceased in healthy ways can be a benefit for coping and finding meaning for the bereaved. Throughout the storylines in the books and movies, Harry Potter grieves for parents he did not know and longs to be connected to them in some way. Although his wishes verge on obsession, his mentor, Dumbledore, reminds him to be more engaged in this life, while encouraging Harry to seek memories and connection with his parents within healthy limits. When Harry is able to connect in a more mindful way to his deceased mother and father, it gives him new meaning and encouragement for the battles in life ahead. There are other moments that touch on loss and bereavement that are handled well. Throughout the series the main characters express sadness, anger, and other typical grief reactions when persons they love die and they often grieve in different ways. Trusted adults model grief skillfully and give counsel to Harry, Hermione, and Ron, while Harry's relatives, the Dursleys, model fear and a profound lack of compassion. The necessity of a strong support group, even if it's just a few people, is a clear theme. The books also deal with a variety of religious themes including life after death and resurrection. Other contemporary movies address grief and loss in valuable ways, including *Rabbit Hole*, *Being Mortal* (*documentary*), *The Lovely Bones*, *A Single Man*, *Patch Adams*, *Manchester by the Sea*, *The Babadook*, *Coco*, *Up*, and a host of others.

Since the early 2000s a number of television shows have dealt capably with themes of grief and loss in various episodes or as a central theme. *Six Feet Under* (HBO), which aired from 2001–2005, is about a family that owns a funeral home. The show explores a number of issues around death and the various types of passing. The episodes offer a reflection on ways a particular death affects others and relationships, while addressing various religious and philosophical themes related to death, grief, and reactions to loss. In the show, characters often have conversations with the deceased, a dramatic device seen in other popular network shows (like *NCIS*). In the comedy, *Mom* (CBS), one of the main characters, Bonnie, reunites with her ex-husband and the father of her daughter. He tragically dies of a heart attack and Bonnie grieves deeply and in various interesting ways, including constructing an elaborate shrine in an empty apartment in a housing complex she manages. When the daughter, Christy, discovers the shrine and notices other odd behaviors, she and Bonnie have a heated disagreement over what normal grief looks like. Other shows like *The Killing* (AMC—several episodes in season 2), and *Dead to Me* (Netflix) explore grief and loss in compelling and thought-provoking ways. *Black Mirror* (Netflix—"Be Right Back" episode), is a fascinating exploration of bereavement and the possibilities of connection with a deceased loved one through technology. In this episode Martha loses her partner Ash and suffers from profound grief. A friend suggests that Martha make use of a service that can create a digital footprint of deceased loved ones, eventually creating an Ash robot. The episode explores the possible use and limits of technology in connection to grief, the emotional toll of bereavement, the yearning many feel for their loved one, and delves into questions about what makes us human.

These are a few examples of video media that deal with matters around grief and loss. Although they may not be the definitive textbooks for bereavement, they offer valuable insight into loss and the many reactions and emotions that arise when someone loses a loved one or friend. As such, they may be of benefit to a young person who is grieving, especially if there are friends or trusted adults who can watch along and help unpack the lessons available.

Social Media

Just as death began to find more space and attention in movies and television around the turn of the twenty-first century, social media has continued this trend. Since conversation and reflection around death, grief and loss have been relatively absent from the public sphere, the forum for such reflection has moved somewhat to media settings. A number of researchers claim that social media and digital memory sites have become the place where thoughts and feelings about deceased loved ones can be worked out, especially for teenagers and young adults who are the prevalent users of this technology. In fact, some who study the media culture believe that social, digital, and web-based media are leading to a shift in the way various cultures process and deal with death.

Social and digital media allow for places to connect online with persons and communities that share in particular circumstances around grief and loss or deal with bereavement in general. Such media are spaces for developing memorial pages or shrines, managing digital afterlife possibilities, interacting with peers and/or bereavement support groups, and connecting to organizations that provide intervention and professional help both on-line and at brick and mortar locations. There are also numerous websites that address various aspects of bereavement and that focus on particular needs or communities (e.g., those who have suffered sexual assault, veterans and families, those who have lost pets). There are some social media and websites that allow for communication with deceased, which allows for continuing bonds and sorting out meaning and identity.

It's clear there are many positive effects of social media that can be extremely helpful to the bereaved teenager and young adult. It has definitely become a place where young people can express their heartfelt emotions, ask questions, converse with others who have experienced similar loss and pain, create and be involved in ritual around the death of a friend or loved one, and find other support needed as they grieve and mourn. It also allows for a chance to sort out identity, connect to the sacred, find healing and seek new meaning. In short, social and digital media provide a chance for death, grief, and mourning to be acceptable to talk about and shared communally, which allows for greater opportunities to cope and heal.

However, there are also concerns regarding social and digital media, especially regarding the way a young person (or anyone) may use it to process grief and deal with deep emotional pain. Scholarly exploration of the connection of grief and mourning with various forms of technology and social media is relatively new. Though researchers mention the many positive aspects of social and digital media with regard to bereavement (some mentioned above), they point out a number of concerns as well. Those who blog about media, bereavement, and particular movies or programs also highlight troubling issues. Although it is impossible to cover all the various arguments about possible adverse effects of social and digital media regarding bereavement here, a few examples will be highlighted.

One of the concerns involves the idea of community and whether those who seek community and help solely through online sources are being deprived of essential emotional and relational needs when bereaved. Many claim there is something about person to person contact that cannot be replaced or imitated through online relationships. A simple illustration of this assertion can be noticed when considering sadness and anger, which are typical grief reactions. As noted earlier (see Questions 23 and 28), sadness and anger and the facial expressions and crying that accompany these emotions give clues to others how to react, support or back away from the person grieving. Unless video connections are being utilized online, these emotions that give simple, yet profound clues to a persons' emotions and needs are lost. Even with video, critical ways to comfort another person who may be sad and crying is lost. On the other hand, those who fear the reaction of others when they show fear or anger may feel more comfortable expressing their feelings in words or other ways in social media.

Another problem involves the private/public question. When something is posted on Facebook or twitter or some other social media, it is no longer private. The person posting may be seeking a wide audience, but at times that audience can act in ways unexpected. There have been plenty of stories about online memorial postings of friends who have died by suicide being violated by inappropriate and offensive comments. It's also the case that an online memorial, or a conversation around a specific need or feeling, can be hijacked by others and turned into something unintended or unhelpful to the young person who started the conversation or originated the post.

Digital memory can also be a problem as illustrated by the *Black Mirror* episode discussed above. In that show Martha comes to realize that the artificial intelligence version of Ash is simply not him and the viewer comes to understand that Martha has deferred the death of her husband, and her grief, in some unsettling ways. One of the concerns of those who study grief and work with the bereaved is to provide the tools necessary to find new meaning and move on with life, while also honoring memories of deceased loved ones in ways that are healthy and life giving. If digital memory programs allow for healthy ways to grieve and stay connected, then it is a valuable tool. However, the fear is that digital memory tools will simply prolong bereavement and prevent the person grieving from letting go.

Social media connections, conversations, video clips, personal memories, and other ways of remembering can also prolong bereavement and grief reactions that might become unhealthy in ways similar to issues around digital memory sites. In typical funeral rituals, the casket is lowered which is a powerful symbol that life has clearly ended in this world for the deceased, even if there is a belief in some afterlife. If a deceased person is cremated, scattering or burying the ashes also speak of finality in this world. Accepting this finality is essential to healthy grieving. If social and digital memorialization acts to delay acceptance of the death of a loved one or friend, then grief may go on too long and become unhealthy emotionally, psychologically and spiritually.

Even though there are other concerns as well, many believe that social, digital and other media can be an incredibly valuable tool for those who are bereaved, especially for teenagers and young adults adept with these forms of technology and communication. However, the concerns are also valuable for helping to discern the appropriate use of these tools and emerging technologies. Hopefully, the communities formed online, especially around issues of grief and loss, will inspire others to speak more openly in society, and overcome the obstacles to honest conversation and healthy dealings with end of life issues and bereavement.

41. How is the experience of grief and loss different in a time of a global pandemic, such as the 2019–2020 COVID-19 crisis?

The questions addressed in this book have ranged from normal losses to those that are traumatic and especially challenging. However difficult some deaths and losses may be, they are typically endured within a range of normal, everyday experience. Other losses present unique problems and struggles, especially when individuals or groups encounter greater trauma and suffering (e.g., natural disasters, mass shootings, multiple fatality accidents). Even though there may be obstacles and challenges for the bereaved in these cases (see Question 12), many typical ways of grieving and mourning are still available, such as gathering for vigils, attending funerals, or offering in person support to a friend who lost their home. There are some events, though, that happen on a national or global scale that present unusual circumstances and more profound issues around grief and loss. The 2019–2020 COVID-19 crisis is such an event. While there is wisdom to be gained historically regarding grief and loss amidst epidemics and pandemics and the traumatic deaths and losses that occur (see Question 12), focus will be given in this question to the events and responses surrounding COVID-19. This will offer a glimpse into these issues for our time and the future.

Although other epidemics and pandemics have occurred in recent memory, the 2019–2020 COVID-19 pandemic has been especially virulent and deadly. As of May 12, 2020, the World Health Organization (WHO) reported 4.13 million novel coronavirus cases in 187 countries and territories resulting in over 283,000 deaths worldwide. According to the Centers for Disease Control and Prevention (CDC), the United

States saw (as of May 12, 2020) over 1.34 million COVID-19 cases with 80,820 confirmed deaths, with numbers rising considerably each day. The 2019–2020 pandemic caused health care delivery to be overwhelmed in a number of countries, with lives greatly disrupted and "stay-at-home" orders commonplace.

The COVID-19 pandemic quickly changed the way society operated on many levels. In the United States, schools, universities, and colleges were closed with class instruction and learning conducted online. Sports seasons ended with numerous competitions and championships canceled. Nonessential businesses were required to close as well, while other organizations and businesses such as retirement communities, funeral homes, and hospitals were able to operate, but with rules prohibiting or severely limiting public access to buildings. Grocery stores and essential retail outlets were open, but with appropriate precautions to protect customers either suggested or enforced. Social distancing guidelines were put into place recommending a six-foot distance between individuals and disallowing gatherings of more than one hundred participants—which were then reduced to fifty, then twenty-five, and finally ten. Protective masks became commonplace. Camps and summer activities were curtailed, closed, or canceled. The economy suffered, and jobs were lost. Religious communities began to livestream worship services, while funeral and memorial services were postponed until a time that larger gatherings could happen again. The pandemic also led to a shift in the way individuals, families, and communities grieved and mourned. Though restrictions were necessary and helped to prevent more sicknesses and deaths, adults, young people, and children alike began to experience a number of significant losses.

Most information provided in this book suggests numerous ways to practice healthy grief and mourning. Unfortunately, some avenues for bereavement were unavailable or limited during the pandemic. For example, finding trusted support is critical for any bereaved teenager or young adult, whether from friends, family, trusted adults, or bereavement support groups. Although it's not necessary for help and encouragement to happen in person, physical proximity and activity often enriches the assistance provided to the grieving young person. Getting hugs, going to movies, or engaging in some other fun activity with friends or other support activities is invaluable. Making eye contact, reading nonverbal cues, and active listening are all enhanced by person-to-person interaction. Meeting in groups can also be helpful, whether gathering at a memorial spot or attending group counseling or a sporting event. Funerals are also critical for the grieving process. However, during the pandemic, these activities and events were either curtailed or prohibited.

Other issues emerged as the novel coronavirus peaked, leading to astonishing numbers of the sick and dying. Usually, those who are hospitalized enjoy in-person visits and encouragement by family and friends. Even the persons who are dying often receive the comforting touch of loved ones or are surrounded by family and friends in their last days and moments. However, during the pandemic, hospitals restricted entrance to one visitor at a time for those dying, or to none. Those who were sick typically endured their illness with the companionship of doctors and nurses, but no family members were allowed. Consequently, young people were often prohibited from being with their sick or dying loved ones or friends. A running tally of the ill and dying was a daily reminder of profound suffering and loss. The sense of grief was often overwhelming. Additionally, the energy needed to get through each day in isolation depleted internal resources for bereavement.

Other losses directly related to the pandemic were prevalent for teenagers and young adults. Graduation from high school and college happened virtually or not at all. Sports teams were unable to play and compete. Friends could not gather in usual ways. Parties, trips, and other special events were canceled. Visits to colleges happened online. Typical ways of life were no longer available, and the wait to return to some type of normalcy was filled with uncertainty. Many began to realize that life would change in dramatic ways in the future. Some teenagers took on adult roles or additional responsibilities in the family, at times caring for sick parents. Other avenues for dealing with grief, such as physical activity, were limited. All of these losses intensified the potential for trauma and struggles around issues such as identity, worldview, trust, faith, and fairness. The daily challenges, news of sickness and death, lack of physical contact and activity, and loss of familiar surroundings and events all coalesced in a way to create a "perfect storm" for intense communal and individual grief. In short, the pandemic and restrictions created losses and conditions that were often difficult to cope with, especially in the midst of circumstances that had not been experienced for generations, or ever before. Unfortunately, the grief was often unrecognized, though feelings and responses such as anxiety, fear, denial, anger, depression, and longing for normalcy persisted.

Unknown at the time of this writing is how the pandemic and the response to it will affect long-term grief and bereavement. However, in the short term there was hope. As adults and others began to seek ways to connect and be community, they turned to resources long used and available to young people. Zoom, Facebook, Twitter, Instagram, WhatsApp, FaceTime, and other social and digital media platforms became a lifeline for many. These avenues of connection were also utilized for dealing with loss and grief. Families were able to zoom with sick and even dying loved ones. Remembrance pages, video clips, chances for virtual conversations and sharing, bereavement groups, and other ways of grieving and dealing with loss made their way into the mainstream. Of course, concerns around social media persisted (see Question 40). Unfortunately, new and even experienced users of social and digital media had to deal with an increase in activities seeking to harm, deceive, and take advantage of others. Incidents of abuse also increased, and some teenagers and young adults suffered greater anxiety and worry due to strained relations at home.

Although limitations and major challenges existed for teenagers and young adults regarding grief and mourning during the 2019–2020 pandemic, there were valuable avenues available for dealing with the multiple losses. In spite of increased misuses and exploitation, social and digital media continued to be a resource for teenagers and young adults to share with friends, sort out feelings, and access other creative ways to deal with loss and grief (see Question 40). Social and digital media allowed for connection in various ways, such as watching movies together online, trading posts, creating videos (for fun or for virtual memorials), enjoying virtual parties, or meeting up with friends for virtual coffee breaks. Access to support groups continued, whether impromptu or led by professional bereavement or mental health counselors.

Other typical ways of dealing with grief and loss were accessible as well, such as engaging in physical activity (while observing appropriate social distancing), journaling, listening to music, and talking to trusted family members in the home. Creating routine and structure was helpful for young persons, children, and older adults alike. Ensuring that home was a safe place, doing projects together, practicing sports in the yard, and practicing a musical instrument were all ways to deal with the monotony of the days and the losses felt. Teachers and professors checked in with students more often, giving class time for conversation and sharing. School administrators and educators sought ways to create virtual graduations and celebrations of achievement. Individuals and communities began to adjust.

However, since the pandemic and restrictions were still in place when this discussion was written, it's difficult to know the impact of losses experienced, the type and extent of coping responses, or the long-term effects on mental, emotional, and spiritual well-being, especially for teenagers and young adults. Research into these issues was active in the midst of the pandemic and will hopefully lead to deeper discovery, wisdom, and ways of coping around issues of grief and loss. As with other traumatic events in history, it is also hoped that society will find ways to survive and grow in knowledge and ability as well as emotionally, psychologically, and spiritually.

❖

Case Studies

1. KAYLEE AND EMMA GRIEVE THE LOSS OF THEIR DOG

Coco was a beloved member of the Walker family. Kaylee, now seventeen, and Emma, now fifteen, had begged their parents for a dog over twelve years before, and when their parents finally relented the family went down to the local SPCA. Coco was a beautiful chocolate lab, but had been dropped off at the animal shelter nonetheless. She was a little over a year old and full of energy when she arrived at the Walkers' house, but a little uncertain after having been abandoned. But, the love and care of the Walker family won her over. About a year later, the Walker's son Logan was born and Coco was attentive and careful around him when he was an infant and toddler. Over the years Coco became a cherished and trusted four-legged friend, a member of the family. She loved to go for walks and chase the ball and play with the kids. There was the time she cuddled with Kaylee after her first breakup. Coco accompanied the family to many a sports game, camping trips, and on vacations. When the kids were sick, she would lay by their side. When a favorite uncle moved away, there was Coco, being attentive as best she could to each of the Walker kids.

When Coco was nearly twelve, she was diagnosed with a number of medical problems and began to slow down. Though the Walkers did all they could to care for her, Coco died a little over a year later, surrounded by the family. She had lived a long and good life, but all the Walkers, especially the kids, took it hard. Coco's death was a profound loss for Kaylee and Emma. Logan was extremely sad too since he had known Coco all his life. When Coco died, it was the first significant death any of the kids had to deal with.

The Walker parents called the kids' schools to see if they could have a day or two off to grieve and mourn, and received immediate support. In the days they were off, the family found a special site to bury Coco and had a little service together to remember, cry, and hug each other. They shared their sadness, but also special stories about Coco. The kids went back to school, but were still grieving, as they would for weeks and months. Kaylee's friends were supportive, some giving her a call or text, and even a few hugs. They understood how important Coco was to the family, had played with her at times, and several had experience themselves with grief. Emma's friends were pretty supportive too, but some wondered why she had taken a day off from school and why she was still grieving. Most who didn't have pets were confused by her reactions and could not understand how the death of a dog could cause so much sadness. Logan experienced the worst of it though. A few classmates began to tease him when he started crying after his teacher asked how he was doing. However, there were some friends who let him know they were thinking about him and were sad that Coco had died. The teachers in each school gave support even if they did not understand the depth of grief. They and the teachers and staff that did understand were a great help for Kaylee, Emma, and Logan.

Analysis

Grief can happen whenever there is a loss and can be especially intense after a significant loss or death. The death of a pet can be very difficult and cause for grief similar to losses of family or friends. A dog, cat, or other animal is often embraced as a part of the family, a companion or friend, and also shares in significant moments. For some youth, young adults and adults, the death of a pet feels like a major loss and can lead to intense grief. For many young people, the death of a pet is the first significant loss they will experience.

It's important, if possible, to take time off from school or work when grieving the loss of a pet. The days off give time for expressing feelings, celebrating life, participating in some ritual, and dealing with practical issues. In the days immediately following a loss, the feelings may be particularly intense and a teenager or young adult may have difficulty sleeping or thinking clearly. Not all employers or schools will be understanding, but many schools follow the lead of the parents regarding time off for their children and youth, while colleges work with the student to decide a course of action. Since many teachers and administrators have suffered grief, and some over the loss of a pet, they will understand the needs of students and do what they can to offer support.

After a loss, especially a death, there are things that can be helpful to the bereaved teenager or young adult. Oftentimes a ritual of some kind is especially helpful, as is knowing of a special place to go in the future to "be with" or remember the one who died. It's also essential that young people know they have support from friends and other adults, especially trusted ones. Denying a person's grief is unhelpful and even cruel. Trying to hurry the process, take away the sadness, or comparing losses is not helpful. Everyone grieves in their own way, has the right to deal with whatever loss they may experience, and needs appropriate time necessary to heal.

It's also important for a child, teenager, or young adult to feel safe expressing emotion, or to know who is safe to talk to. When losing a pet, it's important for young people to know that adults often experience profound sadness and grief when a pet dies. It's also helpful to know that sadness and grief may reappear years later when a reminder of the beloved pet arises in some way, and that such a reaction is normal (see Question 21). It's possible to offer support even when it's difficult to understand the depth of bereavement. Understanding can help with a level of empathy, but being there for someone does not require a deep understanding of the loss, just an understanding that someone important to you is experiencing grief.

2. RYAN COPES WITH THE DEATH OF HIS BEST FRIEND MORE QUICKLY THAN OTHERS ANTICIPATED

The beginning of sophomore year at Simsby High was going well for John and his best friend Ryan. They enjoyed and were challenged by classes. They both made the tennis team, and though the season didn't start until spring, John and Ryan started working out and practicing with other team members. They had many friends on the team and in school. Still, John and Ryan were pretty inseparable. Their families were neighbors and John and Ryan had been friends since they were five years old.

In early October, John began to have constant, severe headaches. His parents took him to the doctor and after numerous tests and other doctors' visits, John was diagnosed with brain cancer. The news was a shock to family and friends wondering how it could be true. After all, John was so healthy and full of life.

After the initial shock, John and his family began working with doctors on next steps. The early treatment was aggressive—chemotherapy and targeted radiation. Though he tried to stay in school, the side-affects were too much. His immune system was compromised and vulnerable, so John was assigned a home tutor.

John's family was great. An older sister at a nearby college called and visited regularly. His younger brother and parents were very supportive and caring. Some team members and the coach would visit, text, or Instagram. Even though John didn't go much, members at the church, his family attended helped out with food and encouragement. John felt cared for and valued. But, John's greatest support came from his best friend Ryan. John could tell him anything. Though it wasn't easy to talk about the cancer and treatments, Ryan would listen to everything his friend shared without judgment. With all the support, John felt he could beat this thing, and Ryan was right there with him, cheering him on. Everyone thought John would be back to normal after treatments. Even when surgery became necessary early the following year, everyone remained upbeat, though John and his family knew the odds and possible outcomes.

John and Ryan never avoided sharing the hard stuff, even when John struggled emotionally and wondered if he would live. In those moments, John would share his sadness about what dying might be like and worries about his family and friends. John was also sad about what he was missing out on and wondered about future events like graduation, going to college, and family vacations at the shore. These conversations were less frequent in the early stages of the cancer, but increased after surgery and more chemo. John got a bit upset at times, but Ryan noticed he never felt sorry for himself. "Wasted energy," John would say. On the other hand, Ryan, in his own private times would scream at God or whoever was listening and ask why his friend had to suffer. John was only 16 and should have a long life ahead of him. Ryan also wondered if he was doing enough to help. Though John never seemed angry, Ryan was. He would not show his anger to John, though he did admit his frustrations at times. When Ryan did, John became the one offering concern and support.

Surgery and follow-up treatments were successful, or seemed to be. John was planning to return to school his junior year. In mid-summer, though, the cancer reappeared and was aggressive. More treatments, some experimental, ensued. School began and John was unable to attend. Through it all, Ryan remained steadfast in his visits and encouragement. By the beginning of October, it was clear John was dying. Hospice was called to offer support. Ryan noticed the high level of care provided by hospice staff, especially the nurses, pet therapy volunteer, and chaplain. The staff and volunteers even included Ryan in their care and concern. There were several visits when John, the chaplain, and Ryan engaged in pretty deep conversations.

John died in early December. The days after his death were a blur. Funeral arrangements were made and John's parents included Ryan in the planning. The funeral was packed. Ryan spoke, and though he felt tears welling up he held it together. John's family and friends told Ryan that his tribute was brilliant. They didn't know how he could be so calm as he spoke. After the service, Ryan broke down when he was with his family. In the two weeks following the funeral, Ryan was quiet and kept his distance from others.

Christmas was hard for John's family and Ryan too. He decided to speak with the hospice chaplain and also contacted the school guidance counselor who had told him to call anytime. When he returned to school Ryan was surprisingly upbeat and philosophical. He comforted many friends. To some, it seemed like he was already over John's passing. His parents understood the quiet and struggles at Christmas, but now Ryan appeared unaffected by his best friend's death. They were still incredibly sad and wondered how Ryan could be this way and suggested he see a grief counselor. Though Ryan felt he was dealing with things pretty well, he agreed to appease his parents, but also to make sure he really was okay.

Analysis

Current research disputes the validity of the Kübler-Ross model and other earlier conceptions of grief work, but these classic descriptions still persist in culture and society. Many believe the bereaved needs to experience stages of grief or that grief and mourning, especially for the death of someone close, should happen in a certain way or length of time. Ryan's family probably felt he was in denial and concerned he would have significant problems later on if he failed to deal with his emotions. Ryan's family was still grieving in particular ways, which may have colored how they perceived Ryan's grief reactions.

However, grief is unique for each person. In Ryan's case, there were factors that contributed to his coping fairly quickly after his friend's death. Recall the discussion about anticipatory grief in Question 24. Because Ryan was a companion with John as he dealt with the cancer, and then as he was dying, Ryan was able to face many of the challenges and pain

associated with bereavement early on. Ryan, both consciously and unconsciously, prepared for John's death through listening, conversations, or
times when there were no words to speak. Over the year, the two friends,
with help at times from others, dealt with serious issues around meaning,
life and death. This sharing does not guarantee a healthy grief process, but
for Ryan, it helped him cope and adjust.

Current studies indicate many are able to navigate the early, intense
period of grief and mourning in a relatively short period of time, often due
to a resilient nature, or due to supports that enhance resilience, coping
and healing. For example, Ryan was able to turn to trusted adults who
listened and provided encouragement and perspective. In spite of their
worries, his family had instilled skills and an outlook that offered a strong
footing. Immersing himself in everyday activities at school and with the
tennis team also provided stability. Participating in the funeral service
gave a chance to explore and express his feelings. Spending appropriate
time alone also allowed needed space to mourn and heal. Ryan also had a
wealth of conversations and memories with John, as well as the example
of John's optimistic attitude and courage.

Going to a grief counselor when unneeded can be counterproductive
and even harmful. There are times to seek such help, but was probably
unnecessary in Ryan's case. On the other hand, a bereavement specialist
could help Ryan process any feelings of guilt or shame that arose because
of other's expectations about the grieving process. The bereavement
counselor (or hospice chaplain, school guidance counselor) could alert
Ryan to the possibility he might experience moments of profound sadness
and loss in the future—like birthdays, holidays, and graduation—and that
they are a normal part of grief.

3. NOAH AND ALEXIS DEAL WITH THE DIVORCE OF THEIR PARENTS

Noah and Alexis were stunned when their parents told them they were
separating and had started the process to divorce. Though they had noticed
tensions between their parents at times, or being cold to one another on
occasion, the behavior that was not that alarming or concerning. Dad
had lost his job too, but was on the verge of finding work again. The news
seemed out of the blue. It seemed unreal, but it was real. Dad moved to an
apartment a few days later.

There were so many questions that accompanied the shock, confusion, and sadness. How could this happen? How could they miss the
signs? Were they too immersed in their own lives to notice? Did they

do something to increase the tensions between their parents? Noah was a rising high school senior and had already visited potential colleges to attend. What would happen to those plans now? Were the parents worried about finances? Alexis was in college and had struggled a bit in her sophomore year. Were her difficulties just one more thing for her parents to worry about? Alexis and Noah wondered if they could have prevented this. Maybe their parents could find a way to stay together.

Their parents told them the news at the beginning of August so, as their father said, they could "deal with the surprise before going back to school." Both Alexis and Noah began to feel sadness that cut deep. They felt as though someone had died, but tried to dismiss their feelings. After all, their parents were right there, though they now lived separately. Anger welled up, and questions continued in their minds, but they felt uncertain what to ask or if they even should.

Through the rest of the summer Alexis and Noah talked with one another often, which was a bit of a change for them. When Alexis was in high school, she and her brother began to drift apart and had little contact when she went away to college. Now, Alexis and Noah felt they needed to depend on one another. The shocking news of the divorce made them feel a little distrustful of their parents, believing their Mom and Dad had been dishonest and had withheld something important over the years.

Alexis also reached out to some of her high school friends. Most of them were supportive, but a few shrugged and said "my parents are divorced too, it's no big deal," and "it's better than them arguing all the time." Noah felt a little embarrassed to tell his friends and didn't think they would understand. But, news travels, and his friends found out from others. Noah's friends started to treat him differently, which at first made him uncomfortable until he realized they were trying to figure out ways to help. A few had experienced divorce as well and knew what it was like.

As the summer ended Alexis went off to school and she and Noah made sure to keep in contact. Their mom seemed to be handling things pretty well, though she seemed sad and distant on occasion. Noah was living with her most of the time, but moved back and forth between the homes on weekends and holidays. Their father was not managing as well, though he was employed again with a good job. He would sometimes make harsh comments about Noah's Mom until Noah, with Alexis's encouragement, told his father to stop. Noah's friends kept up their support and he decided to talk to the counselor at school. A favorite uncle reached out too. Noah experienced anxiety now and then because life seemed so different. He also wondered if he should go to college the next year, or stay home to help his Mom.

Alexis's friends at college were supportive and encouraged her to see someone at the counseling center on campus when she was struggling, assuring her that doing so was a sign of health. Some friends and acquaintances who knew about the divorce suggested it was better that she was at school and away from home, but being away was hard for Alexis. She was worried about her brother and missed the support of other family. She was also anxious at times about her future and wondered if some other tragedy might happen next. She felt a bit depressed at times, feeling deep within the brokenness of the family. However, having taken the advice of her friends, she found a good therapist who helped her sort out her feelings and who connected her with a support group online.

Over the year, both Noah and Alexis were able to work through their grief and find ways to heal. Both poured themselves into their schoolwork and Alexis joined a group at school that buddied with children dealing with problems in their lives. Noah started playing his guitar more and jammed every now and then with some friends. After a while, the siblings found new ways to relate to their parents and found the courage to ask questions that needed answers. They stayed in contact too and continued to support one another through the years.

Analysis

Alexis and Noah had to deal with typical issues and experienced feelings that often arise when parents' divorce (see Question 16). The father's offhand remark when sharing the news indicated a poor awareness of both parents about grief reactions and incorrect assumptions about the trauma of divorce and the effect on teenagers and young adults. Although it's difficult, and often inappropriate to share marital strife with children, it would have been helpful to clue in Alexis and Noah a little sooner, especially in light of their ages and ability to handle the information.

The questions that arose for Alexis and Noah were certainly valid and spoke to the depth of their pain. Young people often feel guilt when there is distress and loss that affects the family, and may wonder what they could have done to prevent the ordeal and pain. Alexis and Noah's loss was also ambiguous since the divorce seemed like a death, but was not recognized as one (see Glossary). However, there was indeed a significant "death" of a relationship extremely important to the siblings.

Friends reacted in a variety of ways, most supportive, yet some who were a bit insensitive to the feelings and needs of Noah and Alexis. Many believe that being separated from the conflict or source of pain is always a good thing, but sometimes being removed from the particular situation causes more anxiety and feelings of helplessness. Of course, in cases of physical and emotional abuse, separation is advised and necessary.

Since divorce affects many aspects of a family's life, Alexis and Noah experienced anxiety around a number of concerns, like family finances, their future education, what their role in the family should be, feeling caught in the middle of the parent's conflict, and issues around trust and communication. Simple everyday routines and consistency were also disrupted, as were counted on bonds that typically offer a sense of safety, comfort, and care. These feelings, though normal grief reactions, were difficult to cope with. In Noah and Alexis's case, they were fortunate to have friends, family and others who offered needed care and support. This was especially important since both parents were likely expending their inner resources to deal with their own grief, guilt, and stress of a marital breakup. The parents were eventually able to communicate better with their children in ways that allowed for healthy relationships to emerge.

Noah and Alexis also grieved in their own way. While some reactions and behaviors were similar and shared, others were different and unique to their personalities and coping skills. Alexis was quick to reach out to friends, yet needed encouragement to seek other help. She also felt that helping others, especially children, was a valuable way to cope and find new meaning. Noah was embarrassed at first and did not seek the help of friends. But, when they reached out it opened doors for him to seek other help on his own. Music and creativity were helpful outlets. What was also extremely valuable was the way Alexis and Noah supported one another.

4. JT SUDDENLY FEELS DEEP SADNESS EIGHT YEARS AFTER HIS FATHER'S DEATH

JT was an only child, though a few cousins and other family live nearby. His father was an electrical engineer and he and his wife were devoted to their son, and JT and his dad were close. His father had played sports, especially soccer, throughout elementary and secondary school. When JT was a child, his father began to play sports with him. JT's father helped to coach some of JT's teams and served as an assistant coach for JT's high school soccer team. But, JT and his father connected in ways other than sports. JT was able to talk to his dad about anything. JT's parents were people of faith, and though JT struggled at times with what he believed, he admired the way his parents treated others and volunteered when they could to help those in need. He and his dad worked on a few Habitat for Humanity homes together. JT also respected his father's work and hoped to follow in his footsteps as an electrical engineer.

At the beginning of his senior year in high school, JT's father was killed in a tragic accident. JT and his mother were devastated. Family, friends, and members of their church were quick to offer support. His mother, somehow, was able to find the inner resources to support her son as well. He noticed that she invited friends and church members over often to talk through feelings and figure out what to do next. JT, though, was reserved. He didn't want to talk to anyone. How could they know how he felt? He was angry at God and angry at the circumstances around his father's death. He began to have nightmares and worry about his mother's and his own safety. JT, who had always been a good student, struggled in class. He became anxious about college. Feeling more despondent and a little depressed, JT quit the soccer team. His mother offered support, but JT wondered how she could have it so together. He refused to see a counselor, though an uncle and a cousin often came by just to listen to him vent.

JT's soccer coach and teammates encouraged him to come back to the team. At first JT refused, but then they did an amazing thing. They created a jersey with his father's old number from high school on it and dedicated the season to his father. JT, overwhelmed by their gesture, joined back with the team. School, soccer, visits from his uncle, cousin, and family members, and from friends at church helped JT to find some normalcy and to engage in life. However, he still experienced deep pangs of sadness. Anger welled up at times. He wondered about his future and missed his dad every day.

Because of his struggles in school, JT felt unprepared for college, and didn't want to be away from his mom. He graduated with his friends, many going off the next year to school, while a few stayed close to home and secured jobs or began attending community college. JT decided to enter community college and deal more intentionally with his loss. He figured that is what his father would want him to do.

While going to school, JT met with a bereavement counselor who specialized in parental loss, and also found a support group. He continued to hang out with his uncle, cousin, and friends. His mother was also extremely supportive and he came to realize how much she had done for him. As JT began to cope with the loss, his outlook on life improved and he gained back motivation for his future. His grades improved and he transferred to the state school with a good reputation for engineering. He graduated with a bachelor of science degree in electrical engineering and went on for a master's degree. He got a good job close to home and worked toward becoming a professional engineer in electrical engineering. Over the years since his father's death he was able to find healing and peace. He even attended church every now and then with his mom, though he also explored other forms of spirituality. He volunteered with Habitat, helping with electrical needs.

Every year since his father's death JT remembered and honored his dad's birthday. He and his mother developed new rituals around the birthday and holidays. When she got into a serious relationship when JT is 23, he was taken aback at first. But the boyfriend showed deep respect for JT's father and joined in the rituals and remembrance, even asking JT at appropriate times about his father. Unexpectedly, around JT's twenty-fifth birthday, deep sadness about his father, memories about their life together, and how much JT missed him, flooded into his mind. He shrugged it off but then dealt with the same feelings four months later when he received a promotion.

Analysis

JT was dealing with the death of a parent and a traumatic death which makes for an extremely challenging loss. In addition, because JT and his father were so close, there was a greater potential for more intense grief and long-term problems. It would have been easy for JT to become obsessed with the circumstances of his father's death, explode in anger more frequently, have a greater number of nightmares and exhibit other symptoms of PTSD or responses to a traumatic death (see Question 12). Because his father was such a positive influence in his life, JT could have fallen into a deeper depression, worried about his future to a greater degree, struggled with his identity and perhaps even thought about what he could have done to prevent the tragedy. Self-harm could have become more of a reality, as well as withdrawal from family, friends and any interest in help or life. However, JT's grief reactions and responses never rose to a crisis level, or veered out of control. In many ways, his responses were to be expected in light of suffering an enormous, life altering loss. He was able to discover ways to cope, find new meaning, and pursue long-held hopes and dreams. Though the journey was a little protracted, it could have easily been more prolonged.

JT's healing, recovery, and the rebuilding of his life was in some measure a result of his own coping abilities, perhaps instilled by his father and mother, or a result of his spiritual upbringing (including volunteering for others), or even an innate resilience (see Question 36). However, there were other factors that helped open the door to his inner resources and engaging life fully and in healthy ways. One of the factors for healthy grief for a teenager and young adult who loses a parent is the response and coping skills of the surviving parent. In JT's case, his mother demonstrated resilience, strength, empathy and love, while also modeling healthy responses to her own grief and pain. It was also significant that his uncle and cousin provided consistent empathetic presence, simply listening to JT vent and share his pain. Another critical piece of JT's journey was the unexpected gift of his soccer coach and teammates. Their incredible actions demonstrated a keen depth of understanding, empathy, and compassion. Though JT struggled with his beliefs and religious upbringing, no one questioned his anger at God—which often happens—allowing him space to question and explore more deeply his beliefs, values, and spirituality (see Question 37).

The unexpected aspect of JT's case was the intense feelings of grief when he was twenty-five. Though there was no indication of what triggered these feelings, there was likely some experience that touched memories and feelings. Although unexpected, such feelings and responses are not unusual. Grief typically lasts a lifetime, though it will change over time (see Question 21). Often, special moments can stir memories and feelings, like milestone events, music connected to the deceased, or another death. When grief arises again, it is important to rely on coping skills and lessons learned from the original encounter with grief, as well as other associated experiences. Such emotions and reactions like JT's are not a setback, but are instead an affirmative reminder of a deceased loved one or friend, and a way to be nourished by the bonds and connection that the relationship provided and continues to provide. Dealing with grief when it arises at unexpected times can also help deepen compassion and empathy, especially for those that may need the help of someone experienced and caring.

5. JENNIE STRUGGLES FOR YEARS TO COPE WITH HER GRANDMOTHER'S DEATH

Jennifer Allison Williams was born on a beautiful summer day. Her parents named her after her grandmother, who had been a great help, support, and example for her parents through the years. Never intrusive, yet always willing to give of herself, Jennie's grandmother not only helped the family, but also provided great care and attention to other family members, friends, and strangers alike. Perhaps it was putting too much pressure on their newly born daughter, but Jennie's parents wanted her to carry the name of someone beloved in the family and community. They looked forward to the elder Jennifer Allison's involvement in the life of her granddaughter and the gentle way she would help shape the values and beliefs of her namesake.

The relationship between the Jennifer Allisons was indeed a special one, and Jennie loved the time she was able to spend with her grandmother. When Jennie was thirteen, she was surprised to learn that her grandmother, who prized her independence, would come to live with the family. She discovered that her grandmother had been diagnosed with something called early onset Alzheimer's, a degenerative cognitive disease. Jennie learned quickly on her own about the disease, but her grandmother did what she could early on to prepare Jennie and the rest of the family for what was to come. As the disease progressed, no one was surprised at most of the changes, but the family experienced deep sadness, distress, and anxiety at times as they offered care to the elder Jennifer Allison. The family would take time to talk about their feelings and how best to provide care. Jennie was always told about the disease progression, included in conversations and encouraged to be a part of the care for her grandmother. A health care aide was brought in after a year, and hospice care a few months later to help Jennie's grandmother and provide relief for the family. But, even with the help there were scary times when the elder Jennifer Allison acted in ways inconsistent with her nature and personality, or when her grandmother no longer recognized who Jennie was.

Two years after being diagnosed, Jennie's grandmother died. Jennie's parents coped with their loss pretty well, though they were heartbroken that someone so beloved was no longer with them. Jennie struggled with her grief. Though the family was supportive and understanding, and a few close friends were there for her, she just could not cope with her grandmother's death. An incredibly special person in her life was gone and Jennie didn't know how she could deal with a loss that cut so deep and left her feeling numb and hopeless. After a while, she began to act out in ways that were surprising to family and friends. She became angry and despondent. Jennie, usually a strong student, began to struggle with academics. Her grief persisted, and Jennie's sadness deepened over the months. She began to withdraw from family events and time with friends, who shared their concerns with trusted teachers and Jennie's parents. Jennie felt guilty about her grandmother's death, her inability to interact with family and friends, and her lack of motivation. She began to feel worthless, as if she was failing her grandmother, or failing to live up to the elder Jennifer Allison's legacy and memory. Even though Jennie's parents assured her of their love and support, and did what they could to help her grieve, they knew Jennie needed extra help. They took her to meet with a bereavement counselor and a licensed clinical social worker who specialized in helping clients deal with grief and loss. Though it took another year of therapy and treatment, Jennie was able to find peace with her loss and find healing and new meaning for her life. Jennie also came to understand that her mistaken expectations of carrying on her grandmother's legacy led to unhealthy responses and behaviors and failed to nourish her life. Instead, she embraced what the elder Jennifer Allison wanted all along, for Jennie to be herself and to find her own unique way in the world.

Analysis

Jennie's struggles might feel a little surprising in light of family support, friends to talk with and lessons learned from her grandmother. She, along with her parents, coped with anticipatory grief (see Question 24) during her grandmother's disease and Jennie was included in the care for the elder Jennifer Allison. Often, this kind of support and involvement will help the bereaved cope and heal more quickly, but grief is different for everyone. Jennie's struggles, though, are not a cause for judgment. It takes tremendous inner resources to deal with a loved one's death, no matter the timing of the grief process. Jennie's persistence, vulnerability to strangers (therapist and counselor), and willingness to reflect at a deeper level were critical to her healing. Along with the support of others, she was ultimately able find new meaning in the face of her grandmother's death.

The underlying cause for Jennie's challenges was possibly a belief she was responsible for carrying on the values and legacy of her grandmother—a responsibility she felt, but that no one expected. Those who grieve often feel guilty or take on unnecessary responsibility due to their own perspective and frame of mind or emotion. Such feelings of guilt or responsibility often arise from unwarranted views of the bereaved about the death and their role in it, or regarding their relationship with the person who died (see Question 25).

Though a root cause for Jennie's distress is suggested, her challenges may have arisen for other reasons. Deep sadness over losing someone so close and special is definitely a cause for greater pain and struggle. For Jennie, knowing her grandmother would no longer be in her life could have been overwhelming and too much anguish to bear. Her loss also happened at a critical time in her life and development, perhaps affecting her identity, world view, faith, beliefs about life and death, fairness and future (see Question 6). She was also very close with her grandmother, especially since the older Jennifer Allison came to live with the family.

Though Jennie was likely on the edge of major depression and/or complicated grief (see Questions 5 and 27), she was not diagnosed with either condition. Her family and friends were attentive enough to see the signs of deepening grief and were unafraid to encourage and support her getting the help she needed. Seeing both a bereavement counselor and therapist was helpful for her, though many who are struggling with bereavement typically need the services of one or the other. However, when both are utilized, it is important that the professionals communicate together in appropriate ways regarding the bereaved. Such communication can happen only when permission is granted.

Although Jennie's reactions to the loss of her grandmother were more painful and profound, it was unique to her experience. Other teenagers and young adults who lose a close loved one or friend will have different reactions (or maybe the same). In each case it is critical for the bereaved to have the support they need. Because of the support Jennie enjoyed, she was able to come to a good place with her grief and loss, and to find ways for hope and healing. Her experience also provided a chance to gain new coping skills and approaches for dealing with the depths of her emotions, excellent life skills for present and future.

Glossary

Acute grief: The early response to loss. Symptoms of acute grief may present as overwhelming physical or emotional pain, distracting thoughts, forgetfulness, emotional numbness, feeling disconnected from reality, or intense yearning for what is lost.

Alcoholics Anonymous: An international, nonprofit, multiracial, apolitical, and nonprofessional mutual aid organization devoted to helping members deal with their drinking problem. Staying sober and recovery is based on a twelve-step program.

All Hallows Eve: The evening before All Hallows' Day, also known as Halloween (October 31); a time dedicated to remembering the dead.

All Saints Day: Or All Hallows Day (November 1), a Christian festival day dedicated to celebrating the saints of the church, whether known or unknown.

All Souls Day: A day of prayer and remembrance for souls who have died (November 2). Also known as the Commemoration of the Faithful Departed or the Day of the Dead.

Alzheimer's disease: An irreversible, progressive brain disorder that disrupts memory, thinking and behavior. The person with Alzheimer's disease loses the ability to perform simple daily tasks, can become severely disoriented and agitated, suffer mood swings and other behavioral issues.

Ambiguous grief: The loss of a meaningful relationship without the opportunity for emotional closure. The lack of closure delays healing as the victim searches for answers for the loss.

Amyotrophic lateral sclerosis (ALS): An irreversible, progressive disease where the motor neurons of the muscles deteriorate. Symptoms first appear as stiffness or weakness and progress to paralysis. The person with ALS loses the ability to walk, talk, swallow, and breathe. ALS is also known as Lou Gehrig's disease after the popular New York Yankees baseball player, Henry Louis Gehrig.

Anticipatory grief: A grief response to an impending loss. Symptoms and features include imagining what life will be like without the loved one, desire to attend to unfinished business, meaningful conversations with the person dying as well as typical grief reactions like anxiety, depression, guilt, anger, or sadness.

Anxiety: The body's natural response to stress. Symptoms include worry, sweating, fear, sadness, self-consciousness, or difficulty sleeping.

Anxiety disorders: A group of related medical conditions characterized by persistent worry, anxiety, or panic that do not go away over time. Types of anxiety disorders include generalized anxiety disorder, panic disorder, social anxiety disorder, and phobia-related disorders.

Attachment theory: A theory that proposes how the principal attachment of the child to the parent or caregiver influences subsequent relationships and reactions to loss.

Bereavement: The state of loss, or the experience of having lost someone or something important.

Bereavement counselor: A therapist with specialized training who assists individuals and families dealing with loss.

Bullying: Intentional, chronic aggression against another youth or person carried out by someone with social power.

Bystander: A person who witnesses bullying.

Cocoanut Grove fire: A devastating fire at the Cocoanut Grove nightclub in Boston, Massachusetts, on November 28, 1942, that resulted in 492 deaths.

Cognitive processing therapy (CPT): A treatment for PTSD used to help patients with mistaken self-assertions that interrupt the process of recovery from trauma. CPT is based on a cognitive theory that persons organize information into categories in order to make sense of the world. Trauma disrupts these patterns, especially around attitudes about safety, trust, esteem, power, and intimacy.

Complicated grief: A diagnosed disorder that occurs when acute grief continues and is accompanied by various behaviors that impairs the natural healing process and daily functioning.

***Diagnostic and Statistical Manual of Mental Disorders* (DSM):** An important handbook published by the American Psychiatric Association listing the descriptions, symptoms, and criteria for diagnosing mental disorders.

Disenfranchised grief: Refers to losses that lack recognition by society as a loss or considered unmentionable or hard to talk about. Miscarriages, divorce, death by suicide, or death by AIDS are examples.

Family Medical Leave Act of 1993 (FMLA): A U.S. labor law requiring employers to provide eligible employees with group health insurance coverage and unpaid, job-protected leave for specified family and medical reasons.

Grief: An individual's internal reaction or response to loss. Symptoms are influenced by cultural values and may include emotional, psychological, spiritual, or physical reactions.

Habitat for Humanity: A nonprofit organization founded in 1976 by Linda and Millard Fuller for the purpose of building affordable housing for families in need. Habitat depends on volunteer labor in partnership with the new home-owners.

The Holocaust: The genocide of European Jews by Nazi Germany and allies during World War II.

Hospice care: A form of palliative care provided to individuals with a diagnosis of six months or less to live and have decided to forego life-prolonging treatment. Hospice care is a holistic approach. The hospice team includes doctors, nurses, social workers, chaplains, aides, volunteers, and specialized volunteers or staff (music therapy, massage therapy).

Induced abortion: The intentional termination of pregnancy by drugs or surgery during the period after the embryo adheres to the wall of the uterus and before the fetus is capable of living outside of the uterus.

Lewy body dementia: A progressive disease of the brain caused by abnormal deposits of the protein alpha-synuclein. The deposits, called Lewy bodies, react with chemicals in the brain which eventually affects movement, behavior, thinking, and moods.

LGBTQ: Refers to persons who self-identify as lesbian, gay, bisexual, transgender, queer or questioning. Other orientations and identities have been added, like intersex, asexual and allied, leading to one current (2020) initialism/acronym LGBTQIA+.

Major depressive disorder: A mood disorder characterized by prolonged sadness, loss of interest in normally enjoyable activities, unexplained pain, and reduced energy. Major depressive disorder lasts more than two weeks and impairs daily life.

Minor depression: A mood disorder characterized by low mood and aversion to activity during a two-week period that cannot be explained by a specific loss or event.

Miscarriage: The naturally occurring, spontaneous loss of a fetus before the twentieth week of pregnancy.

Mourning: The outward expression of internal feelings of grief often influenced by cultural norms or customs related to death. It may also be the process of adjusting to life after a loss.

Palliative care: A holistic approach to improving the quality of life of patients and their families with life-limiting illness through the prevention and relief of physical, emotional, and spiritual pain.

Parkinson's disease: A progressive disorder of the nervous system. The nerve cells of the brain do not produce enough of the neurotransmitter dopamine. Symptoms include shaking, tremors, stiffness, and poor balance.

Patterns of attachment: Characteristic behaviors related to a child's perception of their caregiver as a source of comfort and security. The four main patterns are: secure, insecure-avoidant, resistant attachment, and disorganized attachment.

Post-traumatic stress disorder (PTSD): A mental health disorder that develops after a shocking or frightening event. Symptoms include anxiety, nightmares, uncontrollable thoughts, and flashbacks to the event.

Primary loss: Loss of a loved one or close friend.

Prolonged exposure therapy (PE): A treatment for PTSD that contends with pathological fear and avoidance of inherently unharmful stimuli that trigger trauma memories, stress and anxiety. PE therapy focuses on safely confronting and processing the trauma memory though frequent retelling the traumatic event, and gradual exposure to situations, places, and events that are reminders of the trauma.

Protestant: Christian denominations, or members of denominations historically connected to the sixteenth-century Reformation. Example denominations and groups include Lutherans, Presbyterians, Anabaptists (Mennonite, Amish), Baptists, United Methodists, and the United Church of Christ.

Resilience: The mental ability to recover quickly and positively from a distressing experience or event. Characteristics of resilience include optimism, ability to control emotions, and the ability to analyze events, determine what could have gone wrong, and create a productive outcome.

Resurrection: The idea or belief of coming back to life after death in some manner or form, typically associated with Abrahamic faiths (e.g., Judaism, Islam, Christianity).

Secondary loss: Losses that result from a primary loss, such as the loss of a support system, loss of friendship, loss of the role of caregiver, loss of family structure, loss of feelings of security, or loss of dreams or future plans.

Severe acute respiratory syndrome (SARS): A viral respiratory illness caused by coronavirus.

Sexual assault: Any type of sexual activity or contact that happens without consent. Sexual assault includes flashing, forcing someone to view sexual images, rape, unwanted touching above or under clothes, or unwanted messages of a sexual nature.

Shiva (Judaism): Is the third of five traditional mourning periods in Judaism. Known as "sitting shiva," it is intentional time to be comforted by others and for the bereaved to talk about their loss.

Society for the Prevention of Cruelty to Animals (SPCA): A not-for-profit organization with the mission of promoting kind and respectful treatment of animals at the hands of humans.

Spontaneous abortion: The natural death of an embryo or fetus at less than twenty weeks' gestation. Spontaneous abortion is also known as miscarriage.

Stages of grief: The emotional and behavioral stages a person goes through when confronted with a deep personal loss. The stages, identified by Elisabeth Kübler-Ross, are denial, anger, bargaining, depression, and acceptance.

Stillbirth: A baby born with no sign of life after twenty-eight weeks of gestation.

Sudden infant death syndrome (SIDS): The unexpected and unexplained death of a healthy baby less than one year old, usually during sleep.

Suicide: The act of intentionally ending one's life.

Tasks of grieving: Emotional steps supporting recovery from a profound loss. The steps identified by J. William Worden include accepting the reality of the loss, experiencing the pain of the loss, adjusting to life without the loved one, and creating a new life.

Thanatology: The scientific study of death and the psychological and social aspects related to death.

Therapist: A person trained to treat mental, emotional, or physical illness.

Trauma-informed care: A framework of caregiving that recognizes past trauma, avoids retraumatization, prioritizes physical and emotional safety of the caregiver and the trauma survivor, and creates opportunities for the survivor to experience empowerment and a sense of control.

Traumatic death: The violent and unexpected death of a loved one that the survivor perceives as preventable and unfair. The death may be complicated by confusion surrounding the traumatic incident, social stigma blaming the victim, media attention, criminal justice proceedings, limited social support, and responsibility for end of life medical decisions.

Vulnerable: (1) open to attack, harm, or being emotionally wounded; defenseless; (2) the emotion felt when a person chooses to open themselves to risk or emotional exposure that can accompany healthy, authentic relationships (e.g., talking openly about hurts, struggles).

Western culture: A lifestyle developed from traditional customs, values, beliefs, politics, norms, and artifacts of European and United States societies.

Directory of Resources

BOOKS

Bonanno, George A. 2009. *The Other Side of Sadness: What the New Science of Bereavement Tells Us about Life after Loss*. New York: Basic Books.

Buscaglia, Leo F. 1982. *The Fall of Freddie the Leaf: A Story of Life for All Ages*. Thorofare, NJ: C.B. Slack.

Didion, Joan. 2005. *The Year of Magical Thinking*. New York: Knopf.

Doka, Kenneth J., and John D. Morgan (eds.). 1993. *Death and Spirituality*. Death, Value, and Meaning Series. Amityville, NY: Baywood Publishing.

Kübler-Ross, Elisabeth. 1970. *On Death and Dying*. New York: Macmillan.

Kuenning, Delores. 1987. *Helping People through Grief*. Minneapolis: Bethany House.

Kuykendall, Sally. 2012. *Bullying*. Health and Medical Issues Today. Santa Barbara, CA: Greenwood.

Lewis, C. S. 1994. *A Grief Observed*. San Francisco: Harper.

Magida, Arthur J. 1996. *How to Be a Perfect Stranger*. Woodstock, VT: Jewish Lights Pub.

Soffer, Rebecca, and Gabriele Birkner. 2018. *Modern Loss: Candid Conversations about Grief. Beginners Welcome*. New York: HarperCollins Publishers.

Westberg, Granger Ellsworth. 1997. *Good Grief*. Minneapolis: Fortress.

Wolfelt, Alan. 1988. *Death and Grief: A Guide for Clergy*. Levittown, PA: Taylor & Francis Group.

Worden, J. William. 2018. *Grief Counseling and Grief Therapy: A Handbook for the Mental Health Practitioner*. 5th ed. New York: Springer Publishing Company.

ONLINE ARTICLES

Adams, Jill. 2012. "Understanding Grieving Teenagers." Child Bereavement UK. Last modified August 2013. Accessed December 28, 2019. https://www.childbereavementuk.org

Adams, Jill. NP. "When a Grandparent Dies: The Impact on Children and Young People." Child Bereavement UK. Last reviewed by Katie Koehler August 10, 2016. https://www.childbereavementuk.org

Centers for Disease Control and Prevention. "Coping with a Disaster or Traumatic Event." Last reviewed March 19, 2018. Accessed December 28, 2019. https://emergency.cdc.gov/coping/index.asp

National Cancer Institute. 2013. "When Your Brother or Sister Has Cancer." U.S. Department of Health and Human Services, National Institutes of Health. Accessed December 28, 2019. https://www.cancer.gov/publications/patient-education/sibling-has-cancer

PDQ® Supportive and Palliative Care Editorial Board. "PDQ Grief, Bereavement, and Coping with Loss." Bethesda, MD: National Cancer Institute. Updated March 6, 2013. Accessed December 28, 2019. https://www.cancer.gov/about-cancer/advanced-cancer/caregivers/planning/bereavement-pdq. [PMID: 26389267]

ORGANIZATIONS

Alliance of Hope for Suicide Loss Survivors
(https://allianceofhope.org/)
Alliance of Hope provides support and services for people coping with the devastating loss of a loved one to suicide. The nonprofit organization was founded in 2008 by Ronnie Susan Walker after her stepson's death. The website features stories of individuals who survived the trauma, anger, guilt, and self-blame resulting from the intentional loss of a loved one.

American Counseling Association
(https://www.counseling.org/)
The American Counseling Association is a not-for-profit professional organization supporting professional counselors to empower individuals, families, and communities to promote mental health and wellness. The Knowledge Center of the American Counseling Association offers a wide variety of resources on grief and loss, including articles on complicated mourning, loss of a pet, substance abuse, SIDS, advanced breast cancer, and unprocessed emotions after an elective abortion.

Child Bereavement UK
(https://www.childbereavementuk.org/)
Child Bereavement UK assists children, families, and health professionals through bereavement support, education, videos, and training materials. The website offers information on talking with children when someone is expected to die, when someone has died, managing a sudden death, and providing on-going support such as how to handle holidays.

The Compassionate Friends
(https://www.compassionatefriends.org/)
The Compassionate Friends is a lifeline for individuals dealing with the overwhelming grief following the loss of a child. The website lists crisis hotline numbers, similar or related nonprofit organizations, social media support groups, and suggested books for people dealing with inconsolable loss.

Crisis Text Line
(https://www.crisistextline.org/)
The Crisis Text Line is free 24/7 support for people in crisis. Topics discussed include break up of a relationship, depression or suicide, loneliness, self-harm, body image, bullying, grief, gender identity, and emotional, physical, or sexual abuse. To contact a trained crisis counselor, text "Hello" to 741741.

The Dougy Center
(www.dougy.org)
The Dougy Center was founded in 1982 by Beverly Chappell in honor of Dougy Turno. As Dougy tried to process his terminal diagnosis of inoperable brain cancer, he found few people willing to discuss death and dying. He wrote to Elizabeth Kübler-Ross and Ross encouraged Chappell to visit him. The Dougy Center offers support groups for grieving children and their families. The website provides tip sheets, book recommendations,

podcasts, and school and community toolkits to support grieving children and families.

Eluna
(https://elunanetwork.org/)
Eluna is a nonprofit organization started by Major League Baseball player Jamie Moyer and child advocate Karen Phelps Moyer. Eluna supports children and families impacted by grief or addiction through camps and programs. The website offers resources on childhood grief.

Hello Grief
(https://www.hellogrief.org/)
Comfort Zone Camp, the largest bereavement camp for youths aged seven to seventeen, developed Hello Grief as an online community for grieving persons. The website offers support, opportunities to remember and share good and bad times, suggested coping strategies, resources, and validation of the many emotions experienced through grief.

HelpGuide
(https://www.helpguide.org/)
HelpGuide is a nonprofit mental health and wellness website designed to empower individuals with evidence-based programs and information. The website provides information on coping with loss of a pet, terminal illness, or the end of a significant relationship.

Hospice Foundation of America
(https://hospicefoundation.org/)
The Hospice Foundation of America is a nonprofit organization funding research, professional development, and public education on topics related to advanced planning, hospice and palliative care, and caregiving. The organization offers information and articles on grief and reactions to loss.

International Association for Suicide Prevention
(https://www.iasp.info/)
The International Association for Suicide Prevention is dedicated to preventing suicidal behavior throughout the world and providing a forum for mental health professionals, crisis workers, volunteers and suicide survivors. The website provides valuable information on the genetics and neurobiology of suicide, best practices in helpline management, and use of appropriate nomenclature. The website has a searchable database of online crisis intervention services throughout the globe.

National Center for Injury Prevention and Control (NCIPC)

(https://www.cdc.gov/violenceprevention/)

The National Center for Injury Prevention and Control (NCIPC) focuses on the study and prevention of injuries, including violence-related injuries. The website provides information and resources on the prevention of child abuse and neglect, youth violence, suicide, intimate partner violence, and sexual violence. The NCIPC is a quality source of up to date statistics and evidence-based programs related to violence prevention.

National Domestic Violence Hotline 1-800-799-SAFE (7233)

(https://www.thehotline.org/)

The National Domestic Violence Hotline (1-800-799-SAFE) provides immediate confidential support to victims of domestic violence. Highly trained advocates provide compassionate trauma informed care, crisis intervention, education, and referral services in over 200 languages. The website presents information for victims living with a controlling partner on the topics of safety planning for children or pets, information on getting out of a relationship, restraining orders, and calling 9-1-1. Controlling partners often monitor internet activity. Users are advised to contact counselors through the hotline if they believe internet usage is monitored.

National Institute of Mental Health

(https://www.nimh.nih.gov/index.shtml)

The National Institute of Mental Health is the lead federal agency for research on mental disorders. Health topics include anxiety disorders, borderline personality disorder, eating disorders, PTSD, suicide prevention, depression, and other mental health disorders. The webpage on depression provides an overview, definitions of the various forms of depression, signs and symptoms, risk factors, evidence-based treatments and therapies, maintaining mental health, and links to clinical trials, videos, and the latest statistics and research on depression.

National Suicide Prevention Lifeline

(https://suicidepreventionlifeline.org/)

The National Suicide Prevention Lifeline, 1-800-273-8255, offers free and confidential support for people in suicidal crisis or emotional pain. The organization is a network of local crisis centers committed to suicide prevention by building awareness, advancing best practices, and empowering individuals. The website provides resources and information for youth, disaster survivors, Native Americans, veterans, loss survivors, LGBTQ+, and suicide attempt survivors.

Office on Women's Health (OWH)
(https://www.womenshealth.gov/)
The Office of Women's Health (OWH) coordinates women's health educational services within the Department of Health and Human Services (HHS). The website provides accurate information on women's health topics. The A to Z list includes topics such as acne, body image, caregiver stress, pregnancy loss, violence against women, and weight loss.

RAINN (Rape, Abuse & Incest National Network)
(https://www.rainn.org/)
RAINN (Rape, Abuse & Incest National Network) is the nation's largest anti-sexual violence organization. RAINN partners with local sexual assault service providers across the country to operate the National Sexual Assault Hotline (1-800-656-HOPE). RAIN provides information for survivors, parents, college students, professionals, and the media.

Stopbullying.gov
(https:www.stopbullying.gov/)
Stopbullying.gov is a federal government website overseen by the U.S. Department of Health and Human Services and partner government organizations. It provides resources and information for youth, parents, educators, and the community regarding bullying and ways to respond or prevent bullying.

The Trevor Project
(https://www.thetrevorproject.org/)
The Trevor Project is the leading national organization providing crisis intervention and suicide prevention services to lesbian, gay, bisexual, transgender, queer or questioning (LGBTQ) young people. The Trevor Project offers 24/7 hotline, text, and chat services (1-866-488-7386).

What's Your Grief
(https://whatsyourgrief.com/)
What's Your Grief is a resource by Baltimore-based mental health professionals, Litsa Williams and Eleanor Haley. The website is a commercial website offering articles, e-courses, books, cards, and webinars related to grief education.

YouthLine
(https://oregonyouthline.org/)
YouthLine is a nonprofit organization offering free crisis support hotline. Counselors are available around the clock with teen counselors available daily from 4:00 p.m. to 10:00 p.m. Pacific Standard Time. For help with relationship challenges, depression or anxiety, sexual identity, abuse, bullying, eating disorders or other struggles, callers may contact the hotline at 1-800-273-8255 or by texting "273TALK" to 839863.

Index